Nostalgic

Halifax

The publishers would like to thank the following companies for their support in the production of this book

Main Sponsor
Provident Insurance Plc

Beechtree (Manufacturing) Limited

O & W Crawshaw Limited

Dean Clough

Dixons of Halifax

Fan Systems Group Limited

W Greenwood & Sons

Lightcliffe Preparatory School

Halifax Fan Limited

Parkinson Spencer Refractories Limited

Rishworth School

L Tyson & Sons

Waxman Holdings

First published in Great Britain by True North Books Limited
England HX5 9AE

ISBN 1 903204 30 5

*Text, design and origination by True North Books Limited
Printed and bound by The Amadeus Press Limited*

Nostalgic

Halifax

Edited by Stephen Gee

Contents

Foreword by Harry Ludlam OBE

One of my earliest and fondest memories is watching the lamp lighter weave his way up Trooper Lane to Bank Top, lighting the way for weary workers returning from the industrial heart of Halifax. I would follow his progress from the porch of our home at Hope Hall Terrace as the winter evenings drew in. Little did I think that I would recount the experience some eighty years later in a book about the town I grew to love. In a lifetime which has so far spanned almost 90 years I have lived in just four houses, and all have been within the old Borough of Halifax. As a small child I remember playing on the street near my parents' house on Albert View, Pellon. On carefree summer afternoons we would take sandwiches to West View Park at Highroad Well or go exploring on long walks with friends. The view from our house in Pellon was wonderful. Indeed, panoramic views have been a characteristic of all the homes my family has lived in during my lifetime, from the glorious Shibden Valley to my present address at Trimmingham. I have often wondered if my open-minded approach to life and my career in the Law has been influenced by the delightful open views I have had the privilege to enjoy. During my half century as a lawyer I became fascinated by the processes by which my home town was organised and run. My wife and I raised our family which has been our greatest source of happiness and pride over the years. Family life and our growing responsibilities heightened my interest and enthusiasm for all things 'Halifax'. Looking back it was, perhaps, inevitable that I would seek election to the Halifax Borough Council. This I did, and in all served some 17 years as a Councillor, including two exhilarating years as mayor in 1965/6.

I could fill much of this book with vivid memories of my time in office. Looking back over my lifetime it was certainly one of the high points in terms of achievement and satisfaction, fulfilling the role of Mayor with my supportive and loving wife at my side was a privilege and an honour that I will never forget. Our mayoral duties were a mixture of high and not so high profile activities. Like other mayors before (and after) me I derived tremendous pleasure from what observers may consider 'routine' aspects of the 'job'. Old folks' treats, hospital visiting at Christmas and entertaining various groups in the Town Hall were as much a source of pleasure for my wife and me as any of the so-called high profile duties. I remember well the opening of the new swimming baths on Prescott Street when I confounded some of the onlookers by being one of the first people to dive into the pool, followed soon afterwards by two plucky councillors.

The first Long March took place during my time as mayor. My wife and I joined a packed house at the Odeon for the initial briefing before setting out with hundreds of fund-raisers on that first gruelling trek. The Long March went on to be an annual event raising many thousands of pounds for charity. The Ludlam Trust was one of my proudest achievements. Set up to help discharged prisoners in 1966, it served the area for 35 years until it was handed over to the Calderdale Community Foundation. During the 1960s strong links were maintained between our town and Halifax Nova Scotia. I was invited to travel there by the British Trade Commission to open a trading fortnight in 1966 in my capacity as mayor. Many Civic functions were attended, culminating in me being made a Freeman of Halifax, Nova Scotia at the end of the tour. Less than a decade later, in June 1973, I was awarded the OBE by Her Majesty the Queen in a ceremony at Buckingham Palace. If this honour reflected the service I have willingly given to my fellow townsfolk in Halifax then I owe them and the town itself a debt of gratitude. I am tremendously proud to be a Halifax man born and bred, and looking back over my life in the town I would hardly change a thing.

I am grateful to the nostalgia enthusiasts at *True North Books* for inviting me to write this introduction to their latest volume; like them, I hope you enjoy it.

Harry Ludlam

Harry Ludlam OBE

Introduction

Halifax and its surrounding hills and valleys are our heritage, one we all view differently, but the test of an area is not how we see it ourselves, but how others see it. We tend to be biased - and not always in a favourable way. However, this 'acid' test of the outside view does not begin too promisingly. 'From Hull, Hell and Halifax, good Lord deliver us', was the famous Vagrants' Litany, a pitiful complaint against Halifax's Gibbet Law which operated between 1286 and 1650. By its terms, a man could be beheaded for stealing goods valued at 13.5d or more. A man's life measured at little more than five pence in modern currency - harsh indeed, even by Medieval standards. The main concern, however, was to protect the core of the local economy - the cloth industry - which is where the shaping of Halifax really began.

Kerseys and Shalloons

Sometime around 1100 William, Earl of Warren, was granted the Manor of Wakefield for his services both to William the Conqueror and his son. At the far western outpost of this manor, at the edge of the wilderness, lay Halifax. Another great Norman lord, Ilbert de Lacy, controlled Southowram, Elland and Greetland. The terrain and thin soils of these Pennine uplands provided an unequal struggle for farming, and the emphasis turned to the production of woollen cloth. By the late fifteenth century, the area that we now call Calderdale was producing about twenty percent of all the woollen cloth output of Yorkshire. In 1555 it was stated that the inhabitants of Halifax 'doo lyve by clothe makyng'.

Imagine the local hill-top settlements as one great hive of activity. Almost every cottage was engaged in turning out woollen pieces - 'kerseys' and 'shalloons' - on hand machinery. Nor was it simply a cottage industry. Around 1750, Sam Hill of Soyland employed hundreds of people working in their own homes. His average annual turnover was £30,000 and he exported to Europe. Surely the grandest testament of all to the size and importance of the local woollen cloth industry was the opening of that huge market place, the Piece Hall in Halifax, in 1779. Therefore, what the vagrants saw as Hell, travellers such as Daniel Defoe saw as a kind of Paradise for the industrious. In the 1720s, he marvelled at the vigour of the people, with 'not a beggar nor an idle person to be seen'. Although gone by 1650, Gibbet Law needs to be seen in the context of the importance of the cloth trade to people's livelihoods.

Halifax supporters celebrate their club's victory over Salford in the Challenge Cup Final at Wembley in 1939.

A view across the Piece Hall in the 1930s.

Red Cross nurses parading down Prescott Street in September 1939.

spinning, wool textiles, carpet weaving, silk production, engineering, confectionary making and a host of other industries and businesses.

Beneath that pall of smoke there was 'muck' for everyone and 'brass' - real brass - for a few. Industrial dynasties emerged in the nineteenth century, such as the Akroyds and the Crossleys, who amassed unbelievable wealth, but were also driven by a sense of Christian responsibility. The Crossleys, for example, left their mark on Halifax in the huge sprawl of Dean Clough, once the largest carpet manufactory in the world, but also in People's Park and the Crossley Heath School, which began its life as an orphanage.

'Muck and Brass'

One hundred years after Defoe's time, Halifax was in the throes of that massive convulsion we know as the Industrial Revolution. Factories powered first by water, and then by steam, transformed the scale and cost of production. As early as 1837, Anne Lister of Shibden Hall was noting that 'a black canopy hangs over Halifax'. The outsiders' view of Halifax now changed to that 'muck and brass' image symbolised in those famous views from Beacon Hill - a forest of chimneys and a huddle of houses beneath a pall of smoke. The population of Halifax grew from around 9000 in 1801 to over 100,000 in 1901, by which date it was being referred to as 'the town with a hundred trades'. This had wider application. From Todmorden to Brighouse could be found cotton

New Horizons

And now that the black pall has lifted, along with the withering of the old industrial base of Halifax, what do we find? For one thing, a wonderful legacy of stylish and elegant buildings in Halifax and elsewhere which the process of grime removal has now restored to their former glory. We see initiative and enterprise right across Calderdale in the adaptation of old industries (and even mill buildings) and the creation of new ones. We see a great proportion of the workforce now engaged in retailing and financial services. It is likely that outsiders view Halifax today as somewhere between the vagrants' Hell and Defoe's Paradise, a place that might be associated with a giant, 'the Halifax', and Eureka! - the renowned children's museum; a lively town, full of character and interest, set amidst the stunning scenery of Calderdale.

Street scenes

The area known as Hall End is featured to the right of the picture as Silver Street runs down from the right to link up with both Commercial Street and Crown Street. Pedestrians seem to be strolling the streets with a freedom that is impossible today at this busy junction, and indeed the only wheeled traffic on view is the horse-drawn cart. The absence of motorcars in a thronging street scene suggests a photograph that dates back to the early years of the twentieth century, particularly as the woman is wearing a shawl over her head in the foreground. The building on the right, at Hall End, is a wonderful example of Victorian architecture in Gothic style and it was opened in 1880 by the Halifax Commercial Banking Company. The latter had been formed in 1836, and amongst its directors were the well-known Halifax names of Jonathan and Edward Akroyd, John Crossley and Rawdon Briggs. The company was created from an even older bank which was in existence in 1779-80, and it seems strange to think of Halifax banknotes in circulation - a far cry from the Euro! The Halifax Commercial Banking Company was to be absorbed into a larger concern in 1919, and the building itself became the premises, at various times, of the York County Savings Bank and Trustee Savings Bank. Money and this part of Halifax seem to be inextricably linked, for at one time Silver Street was joined to Upper Crown Street by Copper Street.

Below: It is very difficult at first sight to place this shot, and yet it is a very familiar spot to all locals. Bull Green is the location, with King Cross Street stretching away into the background westwards. The row of fascinating advertisements has been strategically placed to catch the eye of those hardy travellers on the open top-deck of the tram. At least they were braving the elements by choice. Spare a thought for the driver, for this tram had only just been fitted with the 'luxury' of a protective front screen. Change was afoot in the Bull Green of the late 1920s, but it had taken some time in coming. Even as early as 1904 it had been felt that the road was too narrow to fulfil its role as the main route westwards, and that the run-down state of the area made it a blot on the landscape. The growing volume of motor traffic after World War I made the problem more acute, but it was not until 1924 that demolition work began on old property and shops. There were many suggestions for the use of the vacant site as shown in the photograph including a library, swimming baths and a bus garage. However, what arose in 1932 was Bull Green House, a 'state of the art' shop and office development, with a terrace and attractive gardens to the front. Things never stand still, however, and most readers will be aware of more recent upheavals in Bull Green.

Bottom: The narrow and gloomy George Street of the 1920s, as seen from Barum Top, seems a world away from its modern equivalent. The street was just about wide enough to accommodate a single tram track, and proposals for redevelopment pre-dated World War I. However, things seemed to be taking more definite shape when, in 1926, the Corporation applied to borrow £22,634 to buy property in Silver Street, George Street and Black Swan Passage for the proposed widening of George Street. This turned out to be a longer term project than anyone had envisaged, for by 1931 no progress had been made, and any start was to be deferred for at least five years. Perhaps this economy measure was forced on the Council by the expense of the Bull Green redevelopment at the time. Then, of course, no sooner had the demolition of

property begun in 1938, than World War II broke out a year later. Nevertheless the building on the far left of the photograph, the old Bull's Head, was amongst those cleared away at this point. The Bull's Head in which some readers may have enjoyed a pint of Websters, brewed at the Fountain Head, was opened in 1940. The full widening process, and the lay-out of George Street and George Square as we know them today, was not complete until 1959. Thankfully the widening was done at the expense of property on the left, looking down, thus sparing such architectural treasures as Somerset House and the Lloyds/TSB building on the right.

Bottom: Both the fashions and vehicles on view give a 1920s feel to this atmospheric shot along Southgate. There is some very fine ornamental ironwork on the lamp standards, and the fascinating little car in the centre bears the Halifax borough registration of 'CP', introduced in 1903. The 'JX' registration came along in 1932. The real focus of attention, however, has to be the distinctive lines of the Theatre Royal, with its portico jutting out over the pavement. The Theatre Royal was described by the Mayor of Halifax as 'the prettiest theatre in Yorkshire' at its official opening in 1905. It replaced an older theatre at Wards End, and the thread of continuity was maintained by the inscription which is still visible on the building - '1790 to 1904'. The entertainment on offer at the time of the photograph was entitled 'So This is London', and the Theatre Royal could attract some big names. The Covent Garden Opera Company appeared there in 1929, as did Sir Thomas Beecham in 1932. At this stage, the Palace Theatre stood opposite the Theatre Royal at Wards End, and Halifax was well-blessed with centres of live entertainment, for there was also the Grand Theatre and Opera House at North Bridge, along with the Victoria Hall for concerts. The Theatre Royal building has had the dignity of surviving, whereas the Grand was demolished in 1957 and the Palace in 1960. This photograph of the Theatre Royal was a product of Lilywhite Ltd, the Triangle firm with a national reputation and a proud slogan of 'Continental Competition Defied!'

Right: The formidable incline of Bolton Brow in Sowerby Bridge awaits tram no 64 as a passenger mounts the platform. This is a remarkable photograph in a number of ways. Considering its date, 1905, it has very good defin-ition so that the details of an Edwardian street scene stand out clearly - the gas lamps, the fashionable hats and long dresses, and the lengthy apron of the workman to the right. What is perhaps more remarkable is that the camera catches the very tramcar, no 64, which was involved in a disaster, two years later, tackling this very ascent. On October 15th 1907, no 64 was climbing out of Sowerby Bridge with a full complement of around 60 passengers at 5.35 am. As the tramcar reached the top of Pye Nest, the electric current failed and it began to roll backwards. The driver applied the brakes, but to no avail on the slippery tracks. A few passengers managed to leap off, but the rest faced a horrifying backwards descent at ever increasing speed, in total darkness. At Bolton Brow the tram jumped the rails and crashed into the house of a Mr Atkinson. Halifax's worst tramway disaster cost five lives and over 40 people were injured. One of the dead was the conductor, Walter Robinson, who had stuck to his post when he could have saved himself.

National Westminster Bank shows its distinctive lines on the left, but unlike today the buildings end abruptly there. In the background the mill chimneys of old industrial Halifax are silhouetted in the distant haze.

Top: A shot along Commercial Street in the 1930s presents a view which, architecturally, has altered little since that time. The fine domed building in the background, at present the National Westminster Bank but at that time the National Provincial Bank, still catches the eye. However, it is on the streets that the unfamiliar begins to take a hold, and what the picture best represents is a transport revolution in the making. To the right, from King Edward Street, emerges 'the old', in the shape of the horse and cart. At the far end of Commercial Street is 'the shape of things to come' - the motor car. The tram in the middle falls somewhere between the old and the new, for although it was one of the 21 'de-luxe' trams introduced between 1929 and 1931, its day was over almost before it had begun. All trams, 'de-luxe' or otherwise, were off the streets of Halifax by 1940. In other respects the photograph reflects much that is comfortably familiar, not least such names as The Pearl Assurance Company and Three Nuns Tobacco. Then, as now, two impressive buildings face each other across Commercial Street - the Lloyds/TSB premises and the GPO. A little can be seen of the latter, to the right, which was opened in 1887. More can be seen of the Lloyds/TSB building to the left, but not quite enough to do justice to the stupendous Classical style frontage which did designers Horsfall and Williams of Halifax proud at its opening in 1898.

Above: There are a few indications that this is an old photograph, probably dating back to the mid-1930s, apart from the presence of trams and the display of the fashions of the time. Commercial Street here becomes Waterhouse Street as Crown Street cuts across from left to right. This busy junction now relies upon a mini-roundabout to control the traffic, but it was active enough at this date to merit the eagle eye of a policeman on point duty. Traffic lights and roundabouts have now largely replaced them. This has saved on manpower, but it has to be said that their presence prevented some of the modern 'shenanigans,' such as jumping the lights or muscling into the roundabout. The presence of the Fifty Shilling Tailors is another mark of the times. This was a nationwide chain of shops which was courageous enough to state a price as its trade name. However, what you got for fifty shillings, or £2.50, only older readers would know. What is now the

A rooftop view across central Halifax in April 1955 reveals the rich and varied architectural heritage that the town is still lucky enough to possess. Vying for attention in the foreground are the two contrasting styles of the Victoria Hall to the left and, facing it across Wards End, the Regal Cinema to the right. The Vic, which opened as a concert hall in 1901, has all the elaborate design features of its age. On the other hand the rather austere facade of the Regal was only reflecting the architectural ideas of its time also. The Regal was opened in 1938, during that great decade of purpose-built cinemas. Only months before, the 2050 seater Odeon had been unveiled at the bottom of Broad Street. Halifax's first cinema was the Electric at Portland Place, as far back as 1910, but it was the astonishing response to the 'talkies' that really set the cinema age going. 'The Singing Fool', featuring Al Jolson, was Halifax's first 'talkie', and the Picture House (later the Gaumont) was besieged with customers. People in their thousands sought escape to a world of romance and adventure - an antidote to the dullness of the daily grind. The result was cinema building on an ambitious scale in the 1930s; the Regal being a 1900 seater. Allowing for a couple of name changes on the way - the Cannon and the ABC - it still maintains its role as a cinema. Not so its rival across the way, the Gaumont, which is now the Coliseum nightclub.

Below: An old view of Halifax in more ways than one is framed by a shot which dates at least back to the 1930s. Barum Top at Bull Green, looking along Cow Green, is the position of the photographer. The inbound tram is about to take the tracks down into Silver Street, and one of the properties on the right would have been the old Bull's Head. Demolition began on this block in 1938 as part of the scheme to widen George Street. Around thirty years on another road widening scheme, the £96,000 improvement project for Cow Green and Upper Broad Street, was set in motion. The property on the left, at the bottom of Lister Lane, was swept away and demolition continued along the left side of Cow Green as far as Pellon Lane, the Grand Junction Hotel falling in 1968. This area once contained a china dealer, a basket maker, the King's Head pub, a cycle agent and the makers of saws, window blinds and watches. It is now almost totally dominated by a multi-storey car park. Most of the names of these traders on Cow Green, however, would not be particularly familiar to readers, but quite a few will have memories of the business advertised on the tram - that of Sam Stocks.

Bottom: A busy Union Street in the age of trams and gas lamps is featured here, and a rare sight even for that time. The single decker tramcar was one of only six ever used in Halifax, and this particular one stands at the Union Street terminus, awaiting departure for Queensbury. The latter is, of course, a wild and windy spot and the fact that fierce gales there blew two trams over in 1920, might have had some bearing on the use of single deckers. The sign advertising R Thomas & Sons as a wholesale dealer in hardware, toys and fancy goods is very prominent at the corner of Westgate, to the left, whereas at the opposite corner stands the Town Hall Tavern. Known now as the Westgate Hotel, the old name reflects the fact that the administrative offices of Halifax existed in this area before the present Town Hall was built. To the right, down Westgate, lies the Piece Hall, whilst straight ahead Union Street becomes Market Street. The Borough Market is further along, on the left, and the old Lower Market used to do business on the right-hand side, in the area now known as Westgate House. Dorothy Perkins and Tesco will be the names familiar to modern shoppers here as opposed to those of the old local traders.

Bottom: Soft drinks and those of a stronger variety were available in close proximity to each other in Bull Green in April 1955. The Premier Milk Bar was situated in Bull Green House, whilst the Plummet Line Hotel was just a few steps away, at a site it still occupies. TG Taxis were close by also, for those who felt not up to driving after a session at the Plummet Line, although in those days attitudes towards drink/driving were a good deal more casual, with no such thing as the breathalyser. Bull Green House had been completed in 1932 as an office and shop block in an attempt to improve the main western approach into Halifax. The photograph shows just how much the area of paving and gardens projected into Bull Green, providing a quiet spot for a sit-down right in the heart of town. Not that it was always so tranquil inside the Premier Milk Bar, for in 1941 a drunken RAF corporal accidentally fired a revolver in the premises. An unfortunate young woman from Queen's Road was hit close to the heart, but miraculously survived. The changes that have come since 1955 have included the multi-storey car park to the left of the Plummet Line, and two redevelopments of the central area of Bull Green.

Right: The convergence of Commercial Street with Crown Street and Silver Street has always been a busy junction, even going back to the inter-war years, when this shot was taken. One of the main factors for congestion at this period was the departure and arrival of trams on the Hebden Bridge, Illingworth and Highroad Well routes. The one to the left of the picture was just rattling off to the last named destination, and seemingly another thing that has not changed over all these years is the fortifying power of Bovril. The imposing building facing the camera also remains to this day as a familiar landmark in central Halifax, being the National Westminster Bank, although there is no sign of the row of buildings which was to be added later. A current shot would feature the Acapulco Club as next in line after the bank. In an age of mergers and takeovers, it seems odd to think of banking as anything other than a huge international business with a handful of 'major players'. And yet there was a time when Halifax had its own banking system in the shape of the Halifax Commercial Banking Company, founded in 1836. The West Yorkshire Bank, set up in 1910, was the result of an amalgamation of Halifax and Huddersfield financial institutions. In 1919, however, the Halifax Commercial Bank merged with the Bank of Liverpool and Martins, whilst the West Yorkshire Bank was swallowed by Lloyds. The current National Westminster Bank was, at the time of the photograph, the National Provincial Bank.

Moor should remain a 'free, unenclosed ground for the public recreation and use for all time'. Hats off to Henry Savile and the sturdy 5000 citizens of Skircoat!

Top: Buses had replaced trams on the West Vale route in 1934, and their orange and green livery soon came to be an integral part of the Halifax street scene. The old colours have made a comeback in recent years as more than one vintage bus plies its trade around the district. So much so that we no longer feel it necessary to grab a youngster's

Above: The great wide spaces of Savile Park, an area often simply described as the Moor, have been a benefit to generations of local people. At the bottom end of Savile Park a man takes his ease by the drinking fountain in a shot from the 1930s. 'Thank God For Water' and 'Water Is Best' are the inscriptions on the old fountain, a gift to the people of Halifax from Joseph Thorp in 1869, with more than a hint of temperance sentiment about it. On a larger scale the Moor itself was a gift to local citizens, but one which had to be fought for. Skircoat township in the nineteenth century included Copley and Pye Nest, and was independent of Halifax. Within it fell Skircoat Moor, a precious stretch of common land, and when Halifax proposed to absorb Skircoat, in 1864, what agitated the Skircoat residents most of all was what the Corporation might do to this land. Henry Savile, the Lord of the Manor, supported the Skircoat 'freeholders' and in 1866 he offered the Moor, land worth thousands of pounds, to Halifax Corporation for £100. The condition was that the

arm and shout,'Look an old bus', only to receive a deep sigh, raised eyebrows and a muttered 'here we go again' in response. The first bus to be introduced into Halifax's public transport system was a single-decker Daimler which ran between Queen's Road and Mount Tabor. The pace of change picked up from 1925, and by 1940 buses had completely ousted trams from the district's roads. Another sign of change in this shot of Wards End is the building activity going on in the background to the right. It would not be long before a new cinema would be unveiled in the shape of the Regal, which opened in September 1938. With the first 'talkies' in Halifax being shown at the Picture House (later the Gaumont) at Wards End in 1929, cinema-going became enormously popular in a golden age that lasted for the best part of three decades, until the competition from television really began to bite. The Regal has undergone identity changes, having been known also as the Cannon and the ABC, but it has survived as a cinema whilst others have fallen by the wayside.

Left: There is no mistaking the location of Stoddart's Bargain Warehouse - the fingers point out 'the spot' - as this inbound tram passes Broad Street in a 1930s scene. Broad Street at this stage, and for some time to come, belied its name, being rather narrow and flanked with shops and warehouses. Photographs from the 1950s show it as much the same, the name of Naylor's Wallpapers still being prominent, and probably remembered in that spot by a number of local residents. The later changes that took place, however, would create a startling alteration of the townscape. The widening of Broad Street involved the sweeping away of the old property. The edge of the Wesley Methodist Church can just be seen, peeping in from the right-hand side of the photograph. It was demolished in 1968, and became a car park for Town Hall staff. Whilst the nine storey Crown House office block now dominates the upper part of Broad Street, changes at this lower end included the creation of a ten-pin bowling alley, later to become a super-market, and a spacious car park.

Above: Street names or districts usually tell a story, and this 1940s view of Bull Green looking towards Cow Green seems to speak for itself from that point of view. Bull baiting in earlier centuries is a possibility. What is more certain is that the area was once alive with the hustle and bustle of Halifax's cattle market. To complete the agricultural picture, the far end of Cow Green used to be known as Swine Market. The Grand Junction Hotel can be seen just in front of the tower of the Ebenezer Church. The hotel stood on the site of the old Swine Market until its demolition in 1968. Then again, of course, the dreaded Gibbet once stood at where Gibbet Street used to run into Cow Green. Traffic is fairly light on the photograph, but it is still surprising to remember that this route along the top end of Halifax was once the main one for westbound traffic, or for those coming from that direction towards Leeds and Bradford. Congestion had become chronic by the 1960s, and improvements began by the demolition of property along the left of Cow Green. The road was widened and a multi-storey car park was opened in 1971.

Above: Two famous Halifax landmarks are on their way to slow but steady destruction in a photograph that was taken from the roof of what was then a bowling alley. 'Salt' and 'Pepper', completed in 1939, were the twin cooling towers of Halifax Power Station. Electricity had been generated there from 1888 until the closure of the station in 1970. By 1974 the time had come for the two 170 feet cooling towers to go also. The demolition of the towers in March was a highly publicised event, and a cold Sunday morning saw thousands of people ranged across Beacon Hill and Southowram Bank, expectantly awaiting a spectacular show. However, the 50lbs explosive charge on one of the towers only caused it to shudder, subside a little and gently tilt towards the other one. That was the end of it, and although there was laughter people trailed away somewhat despondently. It must have felt like an eighteenth century crowd turning up for a public execution, only to witness the handing out of a community service order! The stubborn attachment of 'Salt' and 'Pepper' to Halifax was finally ended in 1975 by the cruder, but obviously more effective method, of a swinging demolition ball. As can be seen, however, there was now slightly less work to be done on the left one.

Right: A fine aerial shot of central Halifax in 1952 is readily recognisable today, for unlike many towns, the impressive and stylish buildings at the heart of Halifax have not been torn down for redevelopment. The focus of the picture is the area of town which, in 1952, could be regarded as the hub of the entertainment scene. Practically right at the centre is the distinctive shape of the Victoria Theatre, opened as the Victoria Hall in 1901, and the venue of concerts and live theatre. A little to the right stands the lighter coloured shape of the Regal (now ABC), opened in 1938. The Gaumont Cinema's tower faces both of them, whilst right at the edge of the picture to the right, stands the whitish outline of the Electric Cinema. To be completely spoiled for choice in 1952, a quick walk down Wards End to Southgate would have brought you to the Palace Theatre and the Royal Cinema, facing each other. And what better place to meet a friend before sampling the 'fleshpots' of Halifax than 'under the clock'. The large ornamental clock under the magnificent glass dome of the Borough Market used to be a popular rendezvous. It can be seen towards the top right-hand corner. To give a little more context, Trinity Road sweeps down from Wards End towards bottom left, whilst Fountain Street progresses left towards Bull Green.

The foreground of this 1952 aerial view is dominated by the Halifax General Hospital, with Dudwell Lane running below it to join Salterhebble Hill , whilst Huddersfield Road runs off the edge of the photograph to the right in the direction of Halifax town centre. The General Hospital began its life in 1901 as St Luke's, and it was built on behalf of the Poor Law Guardians to house bedridden patients from the overcrowded Workhouse at Gibbet Street. The distinctive circular ward buildings were the 'brainchild' of Halifax designer, Mr W Clement Williams, but recent developments have now transformed the situation at this site. To follow Dryclough Lane upwards onto

Skircoat Moor Road brings the eye to the broad acres of Manor Heath and Savile Park. St Jude's and the Royal Halifax Infirmary appear towards the right. At the top of Savile Park the Crossley Heath School is visible, founded as an orphanage by the Crossley family in 1864. Wainhouse Tower overlooks Pye Nest to its left and King Cross to its right. 'Wainhouse's Folly' was originally intended to be a chimney for John Wainhouse's Washer Lane Dyeworks, connected to the latter by a 350 metres flue. In the end it was not needed as a chimney and was completed in 1875 as an ornamental tower, 285 feet high at the west side, and 253 feet high and with 403 steps at the east side.

Nostalgic HALIFAX

The foreground of this 1952 aerial view shows the junction of King Cross Street and Hopwood Lane and the network of streets, terraced houses and commercial premises running off them. Moving into the top part of the photograph, King Cross Street runs into a Bull Green that has been radically altered twice since 1952. At this date the paved area in front of Bull Green House still projects a long way into Bull Green, with the structure built as a tram shelter in 1932, clearly visible. The Plummet Line Hotel stands at the bottom of Bull Close Lane, adjacent to the area which is now a multi-storey car park. George Street, which runs out of Bull Green towards the top left-hand corner, was still undergoing a redevelopment phase in the 1950s, and the paved areas and flower beds can clearly be seen. Fountain Street runs from Bull Green to what is now the Victoria Theatre, right at the top edge. In spite of a few name alterations, older locals have always tended to refer to it as the 'Vic,' fondly remembering that famous 'sprung' dance floor. One substantial change, of course, has been in the top right-hand corner where part of the old Ramsden's 'Stone Trough' Brewery is visible. This was demolished when the new Halifax Building Society headquarters was built in 1973.

Wartime

A wonderful photograph of 1918 shows the bottom of George Street a seething mass of people, curious to see the weapon that they hoped would win the war - the tank. 'Egbert' was the rather unheroic name of this tank, seen here almost engulfed by flags, banners and people. However, 'Egbert' was not on fighting duty. It was a mobile Tank Bank, resident in George Street for one week in March 1918 as a fundraising effort. Not only had World War I taken a terrible toll in lives, but by 1918 the cost of fighting a major war on both land and sea, as well as sending aid to Russia, was well-nigh bankrupting Britain. 'Egbert' was on a tour of the country as a publicity exercise in order to encourage people to buy war bonds and savings certificates. A glance at the Tank Telegraph Board, showing 'Today's Total' standing at £130,000, seems to suggest that the idea was a huge success. Flags and slogans, such as 'England is Watching', reinforced the patriotic message. On the Tuesday of this special week, 'Egbert' was visited by 10,000 schoolchildren, marched there by their teachers. One hardy band was marched in from Wainstalls! Each child, on popping a few pennies into 'Egbert', received a flag and some got a tank souvenir. Are there any of those still around?

Bottom: A nasty little bug was released by the government in the early days of World War II. It was a propaganda cartoon figure covered in swastikas and was called the 'Squander Bug.' The insect popped up everywhere to remind people that money spent, or squandered, on luxuries could be put to better use by purchasing War or Defence Bonds. The cost of fighting the war was huge, and year by year massive fund-raising campaigns were staged in towns and cities across Britain to persuade people to invest in bonds and certificates. Parades were always a feature, and this photograph of 1940 shows Red Cross nurses and the St John Ambulance Brigade winding their way along Cow Green and turning smartly left at the old Crown and Anchor at Bull Green. This may well have been associated with War Weapons Week, which also had weapons exhibitions, parades by the Duke of Wellington's Regiment, bomb disposal demonstrations and a schools' poster competition. The aim for Halifax was to raise at least £1 million, enough for three destroyers. The big inducement also was that the money was being lent to the government, not given, and even a £5 bond would pay for a five inch shell. Halifax War Weapons Week raised £2,562,939, or the staggering sum of over £26 per head - a record for the country, until Elland beat it the following year.

Right: 'Dig for Victory' was one of the most memorable of the World War II slogans which urged people on to greater efforts. These Land Army girls, pictured somewhere on the hill tops above Hebden Bridge, were not exactly digging, but they were involved in the production of food, and that was the main thing. As an island race, dependent on food imports, the British came under great pressure as German 'U'-boats took a heavy toll on merchant ships, particularly in the early years of the war. Not only were people urged to grow vegetables in their back gardens and allotments, but public parks were also utilised. Passers-by looked on in astonishment in October 1942 as Savile Park was ploughed up. It was in this context of more land under cultivation that the Women's Land Army was set up to provide the extra labour needed. At its height the Land Army numbered 80,000. For most of the women it was their first taste of heavy, outdoor work, and of living away from home, but many cherished the independence and the friendships that were forged. Nevertheless in 1940 rationing had to be introduced on butter, sugar, meat, margarine, cooking fats and tea. Bananas and oranges became things to reminisce about, whilst some children never saw a sweet for years!

A long line of Red Cross nurses parades down Prescott Street in late September 1939, with the Drill Hall prominent in the foreground. There was to be an inspection by Lieutenant-Colonel A C Sheepshanks, and many people had turned out in their smartest dress for the occasion. Britain had been at war for almost a month, and the blacked-out street lamp was a reminder of the fact. And yet, at this stage, the war on the Home Front was a little illusory - more of an inconvenience. It was a nuisance, for example, to stumble about in the blackout so that in the end the authorities had to put white paint on kerbs and the lower parts of lamp standards. Worse lay ahead. From January 1940 food rationing began, and steadily increased so that by 1941 the weekly ration of bacon or ham was four ounces (112 grammes). Only two ounces each of tea, butter and cheese was allowed, along with one shilling's (5p's) worth of meat. Clothing and footwear were to follow in 1942 until the main problem of ordinary households was a constant shortage of almost everything. 'Make do and Mend' was the government's slogan. There was, of course, the 'black market' - if you could afford it. Otherwise it might have to be reliance on the government's every-helpful recipes, such as sheep's brains on toast with acorn coffee!

This page: The Home Guard in the Bull Green area is featured in both these photographs. In the first one *(right)*, taken in April 1942, the battalion attached to the Duke of Wellington's Regimental Headquarters, Wellesley Barracks, marches smartly past Barum Top, with the Olympia Garage in the background. The second shot *(top)* is also located in the Bull Green area, and the insignia of 23 Battalion is visible on the shoulder of the soldier at far left. Parades and uniforms have always exerted a magnetic influence on small boys, and the one here has got as near as he dare. The boy himself is, in fact, wearing the 'small boy uniform' of the time - a little bit different from what might be seen today! The Home Guard was formed in May 1940 out of a government appeal for volunteers to protect Britain from an expected German invasion. Composed mainly of those either too old or too young for active service (and the photographs show this well) jokers had plenty of fun with the early name of the Home Guard - the Local Defence Volunteers or LDV. It was claimed that, among other things, LDV might stand for 'Long Dentured Veterans'. A chronic shortage of weapons at first did nothing to inspire confidence. Improvisation was the key, with such things as pikes and clubs, and a home-made bomb ('Molotov Cocktail' style) which was as dangerous to the thrower as to the intended victim. There was a radical improvement when proper weapons became available, with some training in their use. Military ranks were introduced, along with large-scale field exercises, sometimes with regular

troops. By June 1942 local men were being called up for compulsory service in the Home Guard, with at least 48 hours training per month. That serious duties could be undertaken by them was proved by the fact that Home Guard units often manned anti-aircraft emplacements, such as the 'Z' Battery with 64 rocket launchers at Southowram. However, there was a touch of the 'Dad's Army' about the fact that the only rocket launched was done so by accident. The rocket hit a railway embankment, fortunately without exploding, and the firer ended up in hospital with burns! By 1943, with any serious threat of German invasion over, all compulsion to join the Home Guard ceased. In December 1944 the order came to 'stand down'. Both 23 and 24 Battalions gathered at Halifax cinemas for a final address, and tributes were paid to their efforts. The 'stand down' parade then took place, concluding at Bull Green. Similar parades took place in the Calder Valley towns.

Below: A detachment of the Halifax Home Guard poses cheerily for the camera in this wartime shot, and no doubt the sergeant on the front row was doing his best to 'lick them into shape'. In May 1940 the government appealed to those who were not in military service to join the Local Defence Volunteers (LDV), which was renamed the Home Guard two months later. Within three days 800 men from Halifax and district had enrolled. The specific task at first of these part-time soldiers was to defend strategic and vulnerable points against enemy paratroop attack - bridges, canals, railways and the like. The abiding image of the Home Guard is, of course, Captain Mainwaring and his 'Dad's Army'. Absurd parody though it might be, even in 1940 it was realised that volunteers would have little chance against highly trained parachutists. From the very first, local wits claimed that LDV stood for 'Look, Duck and Vanish'. An acute problem at first was a shortage of weapons. To drill with walking sticks was a familiar routine. Had it come to fighting, most Home Guard companies initially would have had to rely on knives, clubs and spears. Matters improved, however, with training and field exercises. Most crucial of all proper weapons began to appear, some imported from the USA, including rifles and sten guns.

Bottom: A parade is irresistible to young (and not so young) boys, but the two youngsters to the right have not quite managed to keep in step along Elland Wood Bottom in 1942. The detachment of marching men belonged to the Home Guard. Its original role was to defend the country from invasion, and in October 1941 there had been a full-scale exercise involving the defence of Halifax from groups of saboteurs attacking the bus station, electricity plants and the railway station. However, the photograph shows another contribution that the Home Guard was able to make - participating in impressive parades to help raise money for the war effort. Warships Week took place at both Elland and Halifax in February 1942. The specific aim of the Halifax campaign was to raise money to support an

adopted ship, the cruiser HMS 'Ajax,' whose name was forever linked to the engagement with the German pocket battleship, the 'Graf Spee,' at the Battle of the River Plate. There was a programme of parades, concerts and exhibitions, perhaps the most spectacular display being a large mock-up of the bow of 'Ajax' outside Bull Green House. The people of Halifax responded with great generosity, and the final total posted on the flagpole of the mock 'Ajax' was an amazing £2,077,565 - an average of almost £22 per head of population.

Above: A group of Sowerby Bridge lads off on a club trip for the weekend - to Blackpool or Wembley perhaps? Sadly not, for these young men (some look little more than boys) were among the first from Sowerby Bridge to be dispatched off to World War II. A brave face is being put on it, with plenty of smiles for the camera. On September 4th 1939 every male in the country, aged between 18 and 41, was made liable for conscription. Anyone seeing a group of young men like this being sent off to war only twenty years or so after the end of the last great conflict might well have shaken their heads in disbelief. Was it going to be the slaughter of the trenches all over again? In fact it turned out that the greatest victims overall of the second great war were civilians. However, it was no picnic for the fighting forces. There were 588 civilian and military casualties from Halifax and district as compared to 2226 in World War I. Sixty one percent of the casualties were men serving in the army, including Hanson Victor Turner, a Copley bus conductor who was awarded a posthumous Victoria Cross for his heroism in Burma in 1943.

An interested crowd has gathered at Elland to watch this Physical Training display, all part of the Salute the Soldier Week in 1944. During the war people were constantly urged to invest in bonds and certificates to provide the necessary money to fight a conflict on a global scale. There were huge money raising drives, usually with a specific theme, resulting in intense competition between towns and cities to better each other. The rivalry was particularly keen between neighbours, and so there was great satisfaction in Elland, in February 1941 when it learned that the town's War Weapons Week had raised an average of £33 15s 5d per head, not only creating a national record, but beating Halifax by around £7 per head. In Elland's Warship Week, in 1942, a target of £300,000 to adopt the destroyer HMS 'Eclipse' was achieved. Another locality to raise money for this purpose was Ripponden, adopting the corvette HMS 'Convolvulus'. Halifax and Elland had already made notable contributions in 1940, raising enough money to buy three Spitfires between them. Enthusiasm was raised by flights of Hurricanes and Spitfires doing aerial stunts, and intense interest was raised by the display of a captured German Messerschmitt, nicknamed 'Mrs Smith', in Elland Town Square. The amount raised throughout Calderdale for the 1944 Salute the Soldier week was £3,042,565.

There is no mistaking the enthusiasm of the crowd as an unmistakable figure catches a bouquet of roses during his visit to Halifax in June 1945. An enormous audience of 20,000 people had packed itself into the area below Lister Lane, filling Silver Street, Cow Green and Bull Green to greet Winston Churchill. Having provided the inspired leadership that had successfully united the British nation against Hitler, Churchill was now on the election trail in Halifax to support the local sitting Conservative MP, Mr Gilbert Gledhill. It was noted by the 'Courier and Guardian' that Mr Churchill's welcome was 'warm but not effusive', and although the crowd listened attentively to his 20

minute speech, there were a few signs of disagreement when he called for three cheers for Mr Gledhill. Immediately after the speech, Winston lit a cigar, gave his famous 'Victory' sign, and proceeded on his way. Churchill also visited the Calder Valley towns, lunching at Scaitcliffe Hall, Todmorden. Looking at the faces on the photograph, it seems incredible that not only did the Conservative Party lose the election, but that Labour swept to power in a landslide victory. However, although Churchill was enormously popular personally, the electors preferred Labour's vision of the future. And, after all, democracy and freedom of choice had been what Britain had just been fighting about.

Bottom: Some very young faces appear on the front row of this photograph of air raid wardens at Boothtown, but as it was taken at a heavily sandbagged school, no doubt a few of the pupils had managed to ease themselves in. The threat to civilians from enemy bombing had been vividly shown in news reels of the Spanish Civil War, and as early as 1937 Halifax Air Raid Precaution Committee was offering safety advice. By 1938 the laundry at Stoney Royd had been selected as an anti-gas training centre. A total blackout - no lights from streets, buildings or vehicles - was regarded as essential to deprive bombers of their targets. 'Put that light out!' became the routine cry of air raid wardens patrolling the streets at night. Cheap blackout paper could be bought at Boots for 1/6d (7p) a roll. A sign of how seriously the authorities took the blackout regulations was the number of prosecutions in Halifax for breaking the law - 1700 in 1940 alone. Fortunately Halifax and district was not heavily bombed, the worst incident by far being the single bomb which fell on Hanson Lane in November 1940, killing 11 people. Training paid off, however, when a shower of incendiary bombs fell on King Cross in January 1941. They were extinguished so quickly that the follow-up German bomber could see nothing.

Right: World War II involved a massive effort on the Home Front as never before. Apart from working in war industries, civilians were urged to do their bit by joining voluntary organisations of all kinds. This particular body of men was a group of special constables, with a very youthful looking Harry Ludlam on the far left of the front row. Mr Ludlam and a colleague patrolled at night, their 'beat' including Stump Cross and Northowram. He was to join the army in 1941, but has vivid recollections of a stick of seven bombs falling near Walterclough, Southowram, in August 1940. A number of other voluntary organisations were specifically aimed at dealing with the consequences of an air attack, for this was the great fear and unknown quantity at the beginning of World War II in 1939. These included auxiliary units of the fire-fighting and ambulance services, Air Raid Precaution and the Women's Voluntary Service. A total blackout was regarded as the essential first line of defence against enemy bombers, and this was imposed from sunset on September 1st 1939. Street lights stayed off; no lights had to show from windows; car headlights and rear lights had to be heavily masked. Within two weeks, across the country, road deaths doubled and non-fatal accidents increased five-fold!

Action replay

This page and overleaf: That elusive and elegant piece of silverware is being held aloft by members of the victorious Halifax Rugby League Team in May 1939. The Rugby League Challenge Cup had been carried home from Wembley by train, and the scene at the railway station is one of broad smiles everywhere. The Halifax team lacked nothing in smartness either, dressing well for the big occasion. And what an occasion it was! Given little chance by the sporting pundits, Halifax had brushed aside a powerful Salford team to win the final by 20 points to 3 in front of a 57,053 Wembley crowd. Salford had not previously conceded a try in the Challenge Cup of that season, but Halifax crossed their line four times, the try scorers being Smith, Bevan, Treen and Todd. Captain of the team, Harry Beverley, led by example and described the triumphant return to Halifax as 'one of my proudest and happiest moments'. An estimated crowd of 100,000 packed the streets of Halifax to welcome home their heroes in a reception similar to the one given to the Halifax team of 1931, which had lifted the Challenge Cup at the expense of York.

Continued overleaf

From previous page: A specially adapted bus took the team and the cup (with some difficulty) through the crowded streets to the Town Hall for a civic reception. The photograph shows the progress of the bus at the Bull Green stage, with the Plummet Line Hotel clearly visible in the background. 'Here come the conquering heroes', was the proud message on the front of the bus, and no doubt the repertoire of the brass band leading the way included, 'See the conquering hero comes'. The first double-decker in the convoy carried the large, but more modest message of, 'Well played Halifax', on its side. From the roof of the first bus the team received the salutes of the delighted crowds, whilst

Harry Beverley displayed the Cup to all and sundry. People were wildly excited, and one or two can be seen standing on telephone boxes to gain a better view. The art of marketing, however, was quite unsophisticated in 1939, and although newspaper accounts mention the waving of 'paper favours' in blue and white, there is a notable absence of funny hats and replica shirts. The date of these happy scenes of rejoicing was May 8th 1939, and within four months a more sombre mood fell on Halifax as the country entered war. The next time Halifax was to witness such rejoicing was another May 8th, this time in 1945, in celebration of VE (Victory in Europe) Day and the end of six hard years.

These Halifax supporters at Wembley in 1939 look in good heart and rightly so, for the Thrum Hallers were about to record a handsome victory over Salford in the Challenge Cup Final. Nobody outside Halifax expected it, and so success was so much the sweeter. Although no less enthusiastic, supporters were more restrained in those days - no painted faces, replica kit or huge banners. You might sport a rosette, but otherwise a trip to Wembley was a 'dressed-up' occasion. After this 1939 success, these supporters would not have believed that the next Challenge Cup victory at Wembley would not be until 1987 - a nail-biting triumph over St Helens. In between would come defeats at the final hurdle against Bradford Northern in 1949, Warrington in 1954 (after that famous replay at Odsal), and St Helens in 1956. Nevertheless, older supporters will never forget the great team of the 1950s with that powerful front row of Wilkinson, Ackerley and Thorley, half-backs Dean and Kielty, and flying wingers Bevan (or Freeman) and Daniels. The last three were Welshmen and Halifax used to prosper from the 'Welsh connection', particularly with regard to Griffiths, Owen, and James, all top-class full-backs, not forgetting that star forward, Colin Dixon. More recently, brilliance has been provided by players such as Australian, Graham Eadie and New Zealander, John Schuster. And as for Joe, many fans are grateful that 'Kilroy was here'.

London team ended up as 3-0 winners. Halifax Town supporters have been a long-suffering bunch, and there have been more 'downs' than 'ups' since the club's debut game in the old Third Division North in 1921. Nevertheless, those who were there will still feel a warm glow at the memory of that Watney Cup victory over Manchester United - Best, Law, Charlton and all - in 1971!

Top: There may be some Halifax folk who were at Thrum Hall for this match, but not many. The occasion was a game against the New Zealand tourists in the 1926-27 season, and the Halifax players perhaps don't quite know what to do with themselves as the 'All Blacks' give their famous pre-match war cry. However, the local team knew what to do at the business end of proceedings, defeating the tourists by 19 points to 13. The player holding the ball was captain Dai Rees. Halifax Rugby League Football Club had its origins in a Gymnasium run by The Fourth West Yorkshire Rifle Volunteers who, in 1873, advertised for fellow enthusiasts to help form a sporting club. Rugby was the chosen game, and the famous blue and white hoops were adopted from the outset. Halifax was one of the clubs that broke away from the rugby union game, adopting the rugby league code in 1895. The team had played at first at the ground of Trinity Cricket Club, King Cross Street, but Thrum Hall became its home from 1886. A trip to these windy heights was one that was never relished by visiting teams, and how commentator Eddie Waring used to love getting his tongue around the 'r' of 'Thr-r-r-um Hall'. The Shay, now home to 'Fax' and shared with Halifax Town, does not quite have the same ring about it.

Above: It's the bleak mid-winter at the Shay, the grimness of the day being enhanced by bristling mill chimneys and the barren wastes of Southowram Bank in the background. What a forbidding sight for any visiting team! Cold it might have been, but plenty of heat and excitement was being generated in the ground, for although the exact date of this photograph is unknown, it is likely to have been taken during the FA Cup Fifth Round tie between Halifax Town and Tottenham Hotspur in 1953. The game was played on a snow-covered pitch in front of a massive crowd of 36,885. Such details fit the bill very well, along with the fact that the illustrious Spurs team, containing such great names as Alf Ramsey and Bill Nicholson, played in white shirts and black shorts. Town had a useful outfit in 1953, one that had already disposed of first division opponents Cardiff City and Stoke City in previous rounds of the cup. Long-standing Town supporters will well remember the half-back line of Geddes, Packard and Moss, with goal scorers such as Darbyshire and Priestley up front. Town met their match that day, however, as the powerful North

Prudently providing perennially popular products

Provident Insurance plc is based in Halifax and is a successful and expanding motor insurance company, currently in the top 10 UK motor insurers. A highly experienced and professional management team lead the company with high quality and committed employees. A high degree of attention is paid to training, development, professional qualifications and succession planning to ensure that this success continues.

The underwriting business was founded in 1966, trading at that time as Halifax Insurance Company Ltd. It was bought by Provident Financial plc in 1978. Since that time it has undergone two further name changes - in November 1992, to Halifax Insurance and in March 1994, to Provident Insurance plc, bringing it into line with its parent company. In the meantime it has grown to become one of the UK's top 10 private motor insurers with over 700,000 policy-holders. Provident Financial plc is a long-established financial services company originally formed in 1880 and based in Bradford, West Yorkshire.

Provident Insurance is now based in modern office buildings in Halifax, though for a time Provident Insurance occupied the Holy Trinity Church in Harrison Road. The building was sensitively converted, retaining much of the feel of the original while creating a working space for 100 people. The business continues to grow and is one of the major employers in the Calderdale area, with over 500 members of staff.

Provident Insurance has always acknowledged the contribution of its staff to the company's success and, in 1994, was one of the first insurance companies to receive the Investors in People Award, an award it is proud to have retained through subsequent re-assessments. On the occasion of the third granting of the award, one of the independent assessors acknowledged that the company is among the best in the field.

Provident Insurance underwrites private car policies for the public at large and offers attractive premiums for all drivers aged from 17 upwards.

Provident Insurance was a pioneer in providing specialist policies for female drivers and is now one of the leading insurers in this sector, with the proportion of female policy holders being approximately 70 per cent compared with around 40 per cent for most other insurers. In addition, the company is also prominent in the provision of non-comprehensive, second car and older car policies. The company also has Head Start, a policy specifically designed for young drivers, male or female, with premium discounts for those with Pass Plus certificates.

Provident Insurance does not sell direct to the public, instead it sells through independent insurance intermediaries and brokers. Through liaison with brokers, Provident has aligned its back office service to meet the needs of brokers and their clients. Customer Service Groups were created in 1996 to provide a 'one stop' solution for all brokers' administration. All staff are multi-skilled and are able to deal with any aspect of the business. Though queries and calls are very diverse, the

Above: The firm's very first insurance policy.

Customer Service Groups are able to provide 'on-the-spot' answers as staff are very well trained and have expertise in the various aspects of the business.

Insurance is all about providing an indemnity to customers in case of unforeseen events occurring. A vital component of the business is therefore claims handling. The Claims Department aims primarily to provide a fast, efficient and fair service to Provident policyholders. Over 150 people are employed in this department and they are divided into a number of specialist teams.

The Technical Claims Team is responsible for the control and management of every injury claim. Under the guidance of experienced managers and supervisors the department's structure enables staff to maintain close working relationships with defence and claimants' solicitors.

Since January 1998 Provident has been one of only 13 insurers in the UK authorised to handle uninsured and untraced claims on behalf of the Motor Insurance Bureau.

Above: *Prescott Street, Provident's first offices.*
Below: *Holy Trinity Church, following its conversion into offices for Provident Insurance plc in 1988.*

The Operational Claims Team has recently benefited from significant investment in new technology, including an image and workflow system that has improved both efficiency and effectiveness. To enable them to provide a fast efficient service and focus expertise in specific areas, the Operational Claims Team is itself divided into specialist areas which deal with the different aspects of motor claims. Claims are initiated via the Greenlight Claims Helpline which is used by over 90% of claimants. Telephone notifications of claims has improved the standards of customer service by enabling the firm to take control of their claim immediately.

The Accidental Damage Unit supports the Helpline's activities by ensuring that the repair process runs smoothly and that repair accounts are processed efficiently. The Third Party Claims Unit is responsible for negotiating complex liability claims and dealing with cases that proceed to litigation.
The Claims Engineering Team manages the repairs to vehicles via a network of Approved Repairers. In each of Provident's approved repairers there are cameras, PCs and engineering technology systems so that images of damaged vehicles can be sent to Halifax to ensure the motor engineers can validate the claim and agree repair costs within hours of the accident. A team of 15 in-house Claims Motor Engineers based at the Halifax Head Office, are supported by 12 Regional Motor Engineers who ensure that repairs are carried out expediently.

The team consists of highly qualified and experienced professionals from bodyshop backgrounds. The wide range of skills and depth of knowledge helps them to give clients first class repair service. Provident Insurance has been voted Insurer of the Year by the readers of Bodyshop Magazine in both 1998 and 1999. On both occasions the efficiency of the claims process, commitment to new technology, friendliness of staff and being a forward thinking insurance company contributed to them being given the award.

The Chairman of Provident Insurance is John Thornton. John graduated from

Top: *Halifax House on Ferguson Street.*
Above: *Publicity material produced by Provident Insurance.*

Birmingham in 1969 and began his career with British Steel. In 1975 he joined the Iron & Steel Industry Training Board and spent several years developing his skills as a trainer. In 1982 he set up Glass Training Ltd, a training and development organisation in the glass manufacturing and glazing industry. In 1985, he joined Provident Financial as Group Training Manager. His career developed rapidly and he became Marketing Director of Provident Personal Credit in 1992. He was appointed Managing Director of Provident Financial's Home Credit Division in 1995. During his four years in overall control, the Division grew consistently. In 1991 he obtained an MBA from Bradford University. John was appointed Chairman of the Insurance Division in March 1999.

The present Managing Director is Nick Illingworth. Nick completed an economics degree in 1981 and took up articles with KPMG. During his four year period with them he became a Chartered Accountant. In 1986 Nick joined Provident Financial as Management Accountant for a number of group subsidiaries. He moved onto the

management of people and processes during a spell as the Group's Financial Accountant before becoming Finance Director of the retail subsidiaries of the group in 1989. He joined Provident Insurance in 1991 as Operations Director where his responsibilities included managing Underwriting, Claims, Pricing and Analysis and Human Resources. He obtained an MBA from Bradford University in 1995 and was appointed Managing Director in 1998.

During 2000, Provident Insurance won the prestigious TD2000 award for excellence in the field of training and development in the face of intense competition. The event run jointly by The Industrial Society and Training Magazine, aimed at finding the UK's Top Training Team and the presentation of the award marked the culmination of a five month search with a record number of firms entering. The judges stated that they were particularly impressed with the level of senior management commitment to training and development within the company and the amount of personal development undertaken by each employee.

The year 2000 was a momentous one for the company for another reason - it was the winner of the British Insurance Technology Award (BITA) which represents the pinnacle of achievement in that area of the insurance industry.

Above left: The reception area at Halifax House.
Top right: Managing Director Nick Illingworth.
Left: Pictured are Nick Illingworth (left) being presented with the BITA Award by David Rasche.

Provident had invested £6 million over a three year period to help improve the claims service to policy-holders. The awards ceremony was held in the Royal Albert Hall and was hosted by Steve Rider, the BBC sports presenter.

The company is also pleased to be involved in the concerns of the local community, by sharing the fruits of its success with local organisations and individuals. In April 2000 it became a Corporate Member of the Calderdale Community Foundation, which raises and distributes funds to support local charitable activities in order to improve the quality of life for the people of Calderdale. The firm plans in the near future to set aside 'time resources' as well as financial resources to enable Provident staff to work directly on community projects.

The list of other local sponsorships is a long and continually growing one. Provident Insurance Trophies and cheques are presented to the student with the best overall performance in Risk Management and Insurance Unit on the final year of the BA (Hons) Financial Services course and the student with the best overall performance in the Insurance Unit on the second year of the BA (Hons) Financial Services course at Sheffield and Hallam University. A trophy and cheque are presented to a high achieving A level student at Ryburn Valley High School and a trophy and book

vouchers are presented to the student who has made most progress in the academic year at The Crossley Heath School.

Keighley College benefited recently from the donation of a number of vehicles which had been previously declared 'write-offs'. It was a welcome gift as students need to practise their skills on a wide range of vehicles. This action was prompted by the realisation that there is a serious skills shortage in the vehicle repair market at present and

Top right: *Lisa Meigh (Training & Development Co-ordinator) receiving TD2000 award from Andrew Rodgers, editor of 'Training Magazine'.* ***Above:*** *Pictured left to right: John Thornham, Motor Vehicle Lecturer at Keighley College with Barry Street, Motor Engineer Manager, Provident insurance.* ***Left:*** *Hebden Bridge Saints under 11s.*

Insurance sponsorship, and they sponsored an employee in the IT Department who ran in the London Marathon.

In the future the company aims to build on its considerable successes by continuing to focus on specialist markets and new areas. They will do this by continuing to maintain and develop their inter-mediary distribution network, design products to compete in the motor market, invest in technology and continue to develop their professional and motivated workforce.

Top: *Halifax House under construction in 1990.*
Above left: *The Provident cross country team, who ran for NSPCC's Children's Day.*
Below: *The Mayor and Mayoress of Calderdale on a recent visit to Halifax House with Chairman, John Thornton and MD Nick Illingworth.*

there is a need to increase the many different types of skilled staff within the industry. The links with the College extend to the presentation of trophies to the Bodywork Student of the Year NVQ Level 3 and the Mechanical Student of the Year NVQ level 2. The company itself benefits from making highly trained men and women available to its Engineers Department.

The company also sponsors the Student of the Year Award for the Institute of Automotive Engineer Assessors (IAEA) in the Motor Vehicle section of Huddersfield College. This award is of particular interest to the firm's Engineering Department where the majority of staff are IAEA qualified and one actually teaches on the course.

Local football teams with which the firm have connections have also benefited from Provident

Moments in time

I t was hats off for the Prince of Wales on the part of the gentlemen on the left, whilst the cloche hats of the ladies to the right were allowed to stay firmly on. The occasion was the visit of Edward, Prince of Wales, to Halifax on October 15th 1926, and the camera has caught him just as he clambers into the back seat of the fine old car. About to enter, and wearing his chain of office, is the Mayor of Halifax, Alderman W Smith. The two had just emerged from the British Legion Headquarters in Clare Road as part of an itinerary which had also included visits to Ladyship and Dean Clough Mills, as well as the official

opening of Shibden Park. Originally the the royal visit had been planned for May 1926, but had been postponed because of the General Strike. The Prince found patriotically decorated streets wherever he went, and a huge crowd raised a tremendous cheer as he arrived for the official reception at the Town Hall. The Prince of Wales was a popular figure and the Mayor, with charming bluntness, described him as, 'a jolly young fellow with no swank'. What a shock to the nation it was when, on ascending the throne in 1936, his involvement with divorcee Mrs Wallis Simpson led to his almost immediate abdication.

Below: Judging by the two shields and the trophy, these proud pupils have been excelling in some field, but the exact nature of their achievement is not known. Luddenden Foot Junior and Infant School celebrated its centenary in 1994, but this particular photograph appears to date from around 40 or 50 years earlier. The school was originally housed in rooms underneath the neighbouring United Reformed Church in Burnley Road. The opening of the new school in 1894, on its present site, was a great occasion, and it was felt to be real progress that each class could have a separate room instead of the whole school being taught together. The centenary celebrations in June 1994 caused equal excitement, with pupils and staff dressing in Victorian style, and the teaching methods and lesson content of 100 years earlier being recreated. A time capsule was planted to provide some future generation with artefacts from the late twentieth century. Former pupils shared their memories with the children and Miss Nora Wormald, aged 83, was able to give a vivid insight into school life between 1914 and 1925. This was an era when children were expected to be 'seen and not heard', but nevertheless the old punishment book details canings for such offences as 'using bad language', and 'chalking on the canal bridge'.

Bottom: The Sowerby Bridge Prize Band of 1934 must have been a very well regulated outfit, for success in this field not only rests on having some talented musicians, but the self-discipline of regular practices. The sense of order in this band is apparent in the way that even the instruments on the front row 'descend the scale', from the largest on the outside to the smaller ones in the centre. The list of honours is impressive and the bandsmen include, at far right on the second row, Mr · Arthur Throp. Great-grandfather of local historian, Stephen Gee, Mr Throp was one of the best flugel horn players in the country. He also played for King Cross Band and later was to become bandmaster of the Sowerby Bridge Prize Band.

Brass bands are woven into the cultural fabric of the North, and a Brass Band Heritage trust was set up in 1996. Unfortunately, the old Hovis advertisements, with the camera lingering lovingly over cobbled streets, accompanied by the strains of a brass band, only presented a quaint, 'folksy' image. Even Brighouse and Rastrick's successful version of the 'Floral Dance' was regarded as no more than a curiosity nationally. It took the rather more robust approach of the film 'Brassed Off' to present the world of brass bands in a realistic and unsentimental setting.

It's a nice sunny day in Hebden Bridge, possibly in the 1940s, and clearly some sort of outing for the youngsters is on the cards. Perhaps they were going to form part of a carnival or anniversary procession. Most towns have seen a lot of changes since the end of World War II, but few can have changed as much as Hebden Bridge.

'Fustianopolis' was once its nickname. A home to sewing shops and ready-made clothing, clogs and cobbled streets, it was a thriving little manufacturing town. Then economic change began to bite, and the mills began to close. By around 1960 the place seemed moribund, a population in decline as young people left in droves. Regeneration began

when a group of local people set up a Civic Trust. Accepting that large-scale manufacturing was unlikely ever to return, the aim became to exploit the natural advantages of Hebden Bridge - a town of historical interest set in surroundings of outstanding natural beauty. Stone cleaning worked wonders on the houses clambering up the hillsides, and the clearer atmosphere enhanced the effect. And so the modern Hebden Bridge was born- tourists, 'alternative lifestyles,' arts festivals and a touch of the quaint. This scenario may not have entirely astonished the 'Hebden Briggers' on the photograph. Day-trippers have been flocking to Hardcastle Crags for over 100 years.

King George VI and Queen Elizabeth made only the most fleeting of appearances in Brighouse on October 20th 1937, but nevertheless large and enthusiastic crowds were there to greet them. The occasion formed part of a tour of Yorkshire's industrial centres by the royal couple. After spending two hours in Halifax, the royal party's motor cavalcade proceeded through Halifax town centre, and then on through Elland and Brighouse. As the photograph shows, there were plenty of youngsters lining the streets of Brighouse awaiting a glimpse of their majesties, and although the wait probably seemed a long one, the Union Jacks were put to good use when the time came. After all, in a world without television, important figures had to be seen in the flesh or not at all. It was around 2.45pm when the Brighouse and Rastrick Band struck up with the National Anthem. A triumphal arch had been erected near the Rawson Arms to mark the entry into Brighouse, and all along the road from the Education Offices to Bonegate, via Commercial Street, the royal car moved slowly between cheering crowds, whose enthusiasm was duly acknowledged by the King and Queen. Then the cavalcade speeded up towards Bailiff Bridge and was gone. Brief though the experience had been, one Brighouse lady probably summed up the feelings of many when she said,'I wouldn't have missed it for anything'.

detachment of the British Red Cross Society. At a ceremony on the lawn she then presented first aid, nursing and proficiency certificates, along with some three years' service badges. Three rousing cheers were given to the Princess Royal at her departure, and she found time to visit the Royal Halifax Infirmary on her way home.

Top: People's Park may well have better days ahead once again, but there was no doubt of its huge popularity in the 1930s, as shown in this photograph. There is a good attendance for the imminent concert at the bandstand, and the display of period fashion on view is very arresting. It is very much a 'dressed up' occasion, and on the terrace it's the old, old story - the young men admiring the girls. People's Park was one of several gifts to the citizens of Halifax by the Crossley family. When the family's carpet mills at Dean Clough were founded in 1802 by John Crossley, his wife Martha famously stated, 'If the Lord does bless us at this place, the poor shall taste of it'. Their three sons - John, Joseph and Francis - put aside one tenth of their profits for philanthropic purposes. People's Park was the outcome of the vision of Francis Crossley and the creative skills of Sir Joseph Paxton. Just over 12 barren acres were transformed into beautiful parkland with trees, shrubs, flowerbeds, rockeries, ponds, a fountain, winding paths and classical statuary. Francis Crossley's gift was opened with great ceremony in 1857, and ten years later he gave an endowment to help the Corporation with the upkeep of the park. A statue of Sir Francis Crossley was erected in the pavilion in 1860, and the bandstand was added in 1879.

Above: Red Cross nurses eagerly inspect their various certificates whilst not being entirely unaware that the camera is on them. This cheerful scene was captured outside the Princess Mary High School in July 1940, a time when it may have been difficult to look on the bright side. This was Britain's 'darkest hour', standing alone with Hitler poised to invade, although within two months it was to become Britain's 'finest hour', with the gallant Battle of Britain pilots winning control of the skies. Nevertheless it had to be business as usual, and in July 1940 the Princess Royal made a visit to Halifax in her capacity as Commandant-in-Chief of the British Red Cross Society. She visited first the headquarters of the Halifax YMCA in Union Street, where she chatted freely to soldiers and staff, and expressed her admiration of the work being done by the YMCA for the comfort of soldiers. The Princess Royal then proceeded to the Princess Mary High School where she inspected almost 200 officers and nurses of the Halifax

You can almost smell the delicious aromas that would have been wafting across Savile Park as the Mayor of Halifax makes the first ceremonial incision in the roasted ox. Behind him stands the Mayoress, and amongst the white-coated butchers who would have been applying their expertise to the task was a Mr Ludlam, the father of the well-known local figure Harry Ludlam. The ox-roast was just one feature of this particular Royal Infirmary Gala, an annual event to raise funds. The Royal Halifax Infirmary had been run as a charity hospital since its opening in 1808, and until the formation of the National Health Service in 1948 it relied heavily on bequests, gifts and continuous fund-raising. The annual gala was probably the biggest single event in this respect, and was an important feature of the social calendar for Halifax people. The 1930s is the likely date of this photograph, and linked with the event was the election of the Gala Queen. Generous Cash gifts were sometimes given also. In 1938 Mrs Ada Ward presented £10,000 for the building of the Arthur and Ada Ward. The largest single bequest was that of Mr AS Macrae who, in 1945, left £50,000 to the Infirmary, along with his home (Warley House) and grounds.

never before. The austerity of the immediate post-war years had ended, and ordinary families could think in terms of washing machines, refrigerators, televisions - even cars. Harold MacMillan often gave the impression that politics was a huge joke, but behind this apparent detachment there lurked a shrewd political brain.

Top: No sooner had World War II ended, in 1945, than Britain became involved in the Cold War with Russia. The prospect of a nuclear attack and the possible destruction of essential public services became a terrifying possibility. Images of Hiroshima planted a fatalistic belief in the minds of some that nuclear war offered

Above: One very famous national figure, and some well-known local faces, are sharing this platform in 1959. Prime Minister Harold MacMillan appears to be adjusting his tie after making a comment that has obviously tickled the fancy of Frank Swire. Further to the right, Maurice MacMillan is not so sure, whilst to the left Katie MacMillan and Harry Ludlam are 'playing a straight bat'. The occasion was the lead up to the general election of October 1959, and the Prime Minister was appearing in Halifax in support of his son, Maurice, the sitting Conservative MP. Harold MacMillan was one of the more charismatic of post-war Prime Ministers, immortalised in the famous cartoon of him as 'Supermac'. It has been said that the phrase, 'You've never had it so good', is a misquotation, but once again it attaches itself indelibly to the man. What became a catch-phrase also contained some truth, for in the later 1950s the living standards of British people began to rise as

either death or a world that was not worth surviving in. The government felt, however, that through Civil Defence a complete breakdown of services could be avoided in the event of a crisis. This cheerful group at Birkenshaw contained three members of the Halifax branch of Civil Defence, as their badges show. Mrs L Hainsworth holds out the plate and behind her, from left to right, stand Mr FT Stubbings, Mr G Varley and Police Inspector RE Baldwin. The date, 1956, suggests that this was one of a series of Civil Defence Emergency Feeding exercises that were being held around the country at this time. The Women's Voluntary Service was often involved in these and it became renowned for rustling up hundreds of meals on improvised dustbin ovens and brick hotplate stoves in the open air. Not only this, the expertise gained by civilian volunteers in such areas as fire-fighting and ambulance work during the recent war was felt to be of value in these still dangerous times.

Everything and everybody is looking clean, shiny and well-scrubbed, including the Mayor's car, outside the Halifax Citadel in July 1965. The Mayor, Councillor H Ludlam JP, and the Mayoress Mrs Ludlam, look in relaxed mood in the background. The children, perhaps less well versed in appearing before a camera, appear somewhat self-conscious. The Salvation Army girls, however, look absolutely splendid in their bonnets and uniforms. Meanwhile a Salvation Army parade was winding its way through the streets towards the Citadel for a special centenary service, and the pictured group was awaiting its arrival. Halifax had close links with the founder of the Salvation Army, General William Booth, who had first come to the town in 1856 as a minister of the Methodist New Connexion at Salem Chapel. He then went on to work among the poor of London, founding his Salvation Army in 1878. General Booth returned three times on visits to Halifax, the third occasion being in 1905 when he was accompanied by his son Bramwell, who took over the organisation in 1912 at his father's death. Bramwell had been born at Gerrard Street, Halifax, and in 1926 he was presented with a silver casket on being made a Freeman of Halifax. Bramwell House, a Salvation Army hostel for men, existed for many years at Carlton Place.

Above: The lot of a mayor and mayoress is a very busy one, and even more so as Christmas time approaches, although it must be uplifting to share in the festive spirits of so many groups of people. The Mayor and Mayoress of Halifax, Councillor and Mrs H Ludlam, were the guests of Warley Darby and Joan Club in December 1965 for the Christmas party. A cracker is about to be pulled, and the Mayor proposed a toast to the club. After tea, the club members settled down to what seems to have been an excellent evening's entertainment. Children of Warley Town School sang carols, under the direction of Mr D Armitage, accompanied on the accordion by the Headmaster, Richard Marsden. This was sure to have been a hit with the senior citizens. Community singing followed, and then entertainment was provided by Mr and Mrs Stanley Williams, Mr Ivor Richardson, Miss Shirley Peel, Mr Harry Dawson and Miss Pauline Law; all-in-all a 'gradely do'. As for Councillor and Mrs Ludlam, they had already spent the afternoon at the Head Post Office and the overflow sorting office at the Drill Hall, seeing how the huge volumes of Christmas mail were dealt with. Certainly a busy life!

Above right: The general election campaign of 1959 saw the sitting Halifax MP, Maurice MacMillan, attract a few political 'heavyweights' in support of his efforts to retain the seat. His father, Prime Minister Harold MacMillan, was one of these, as was the familiar figure of Reginald Maudling, on the far right of the photograph. Mr MacMillan's wife, Katie, stands between the two, whilst at far left Mr Harry Ludlam is also sporting Conservative 'favours'. Maurice MacMillan had won the marginal seat of Halifax in 1955, defeating Dryden Brook, who had held the town for Labour for the previous ten years. Mr MacMillan, an only son, was educated at Eton and Oxford University, and followed his father into politics after distinguished war service. He was given a political 'baptism of fire' in 1945, contesting the rock solid Labour constituency of Seaham Harbour against the formidable Emmanuel Shinwell. He also contested Lincoln and Wakefield before finding favour with the electorate of Halifax. Mr MacMillan held the seat until 1964 and later, as MP for Farnham, he became Employment Minister and Paymaster General. He never forgot his Halifax links, and on being raised to the peerage in 1984, he chose the title of Viscount MacMillan of Ovenden. He died the same year, aged 63.

This page: It is unlikely that anyone who has not experienced it can fully appreciate the hectic life of a mayor and mayoress. During his year in the mayoral office, 1965 to 1966, Councillor H Ludlam JP fulfilled 170 engagements. His wife, Mayoress Mrs Ludlam, undertook 157. Jointly they did 239, thus reaching a grand total of 566 engagements. Had they done a mere one a day, numerous organisations in the Halifax borough might well have felt left out. These two photographs reveal a tiny slice of this busy year. The first one *(bottom)* was taken at the opening of the Illingworth Mother and Baby Club in October 1965, whilst the second one *(below)* shows Councillor and Mrs Ludlam on a visit to Northowram Hall Hospital. Whilst the latter probably had to be pretty much of a 'hands off ' tour, the scene at Illingworth captures Mrs Ludlam very much in the thick of the action with the mothers and babies. She

has a friendly arm around young Robyn Watson, but it looks as if it is going to be a struggle to prevent baby Andrew from emptying the contents of her handbag all over the floor! Mrs Joan Watson holds Andrew, and to the right of her is a smiling Mrs Mavis Elsworth, with Jennifer. The rest of the mothers at this happy, if hectic event, were Mrs Ann Smith, with Andrea and Lesley, Mrs Elaine Bates with Diane, and at far right, Mrs Norma Dewhirst holding Barbara. Young mums of the 1960s were not content to stay at home and listen to 'Woman's Hour'. They got together and formed mother and baby clubs, toddlers' clubs and playgroups. They are still going strong today, and not only do such initiatives give pre-school children the opportunity to learn social skills through play activities, they allow mothers to form mutually supportive networks. Every one of the 566 engagements of the Mayor and

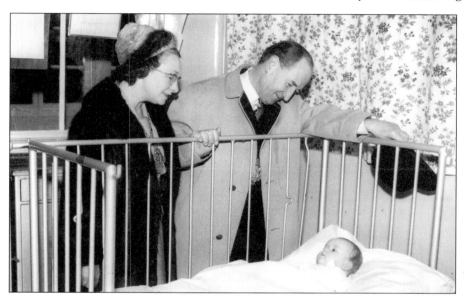

Mayoress of Halifax between 1965 and 1966 had its own significance, but clearly there were highlights for Councillor Ludlam and Mrs Ludlam. The visit of King Peter of Yugoslavia, and the invitation to attend the installation of the Duchess of Kent as Chancellor of Leeds University, must have been memorable. But so too was the opening of the new baths on Prescott Street, when the Mayor and three councillors 'made a splash' by diving in. Whether it was visiting Halifax, Nova Scotia, or opening the Sporting Life public house at Wheatley, it was all part and parcel of the mayoral year.

Bottom: The exact nature of this occasion at Barkisland Junior and Infant School is not known, but the presence of choristers, parents and a band suggests that it was an important one. Christ Church is the likely destination of the procession, and as the church and school have always been closely associated, possibly this event was part of the centenary celebrations of Christ Church in 1954. Barkisland was in the Diocese of Ripon in 1854, and so it was the Bishop of Ripon who consecrated Christ Church at this date. The village merited a new church, one more suited to the mid-nineteenth century population of around 2000. In the fourteenth century it is reckoned that the population was around 95! The church had been connected with the old grammar school, which closed in 1860, and the new elementary school, which opened at Barkisland in 1868, was a church foundation. Figures from 1875 show a thriving Christ Church Sunday School with 250 scholars and teachers. At the centenary of the laying of the foundation stone, Archdeacon Treacy (of railway fame) conducted the service. The Krumlin Band is leading the procession on the photograph. Unfortunately, in the minds of many, the brass band would not represent the links between Krumlin and music, rather the disastrous pop festival washed away by the weather in 1970.

Right: It's a wet day in Elland, and the umbrellas are on duty, but the weather has not deterred people from attending an important event in their lives, and one for which many had worked very hard. The occasion was the laying of the foundation stone of St Patrick's Roman Catholic Church in Victoria Road. The opening ceremony at St Patrick's took place in October 1960, the dedication being performed by the Bishop of Leeds, Dr GP Dwyer. About 40 priests attended the service, including the Reverend FO McNally, parish priest of the new church. Chairman of the Elland Urban District Council, Councillor W Ramsden was present, along with other council members. The congregation packed the new church and several people had to listen to the service from the porch and the doorway. The old church was situated on Green Lane, West Vale, and it was children from St Patrick's School, West Vale, who led the singing. Over 40 years on, and much has altered in the scene shown by the photograph. The imposing building of St Patrick's, with the large crucifixion scene on a glass background, dominates the spot, and the neighbouring garage is now the Thrust Service Station. At the opening ceremony, those left outside could at least appreciate the impressive frontage, for the building was floodlit.

On the move

A busy scene, and a very labour intensive one, at the junction of Cow Green with Pellon Lane and Broad Street. There seems to be not one piece of mechanical equipment in sight as a large group of 'navvies' labours away at re-laying the tram track. The Ebenezer Church is a prominent landmark facing the camera, whilst the old Grand Junction Hotel (demolished in 1968) makes its presence felt at the left edge. A few interested onlookers watch on, as always used to be the case when roads were dug up. This no longer seems to apply. Perhaps we have become more sophisticated in our 'entertainments', or perhaps the pace of life no longer allows us to 'stand and stare'. The photograph gives some indication of just how much investment went into building and maintaining a tramway system. There were not only the tracks, but also the power line system. Steam driven generators at Halifax Electricity Works drove the system, and power cuts could sometimes prove problematic. These must have numbered among the reasons why buses began to take over from trams in the 1930s. The tram network shrank until the last tram ran in 1939. Buses were more flexible and more economic to run. Once you had built them, the infrastructure was already there - the roads.

Above: They didn't mince their words in the 1930s. No such niceties as 'Slow - Danger'; the bald statement on the lamp standard to the left is 'Death Trap'. It is easy to see why, for Fallingroyd Bridge, between Mytholmroyd and Hebden Bridge, took an almost 90 degrees turn in those days. Even at the speed vehicles pottered along at then, the bridge had clearly claimed some victims. Much work has been done since then at Fallingroyd to re-align the road and modify the bend, but at the same time cars have become capable of much greater speeds. Nevertheless the bridge does not quite have the bad reputation it used to have. There was no particular problem for trams at this point. It was steep hills which could be their undoing, and as Halifax had just about the hilliest tramway system in Britain, it was perhaps not surprising that between 1898 (the opening of the system) and 1917 there were six accidents involving runaway trams on hills. Some of these had caused fatalities. For the tram pictured, Hebden Bridge was literally the end of the line, for the system ran no further westwards. Even to get so far, the power had to be boosted by a sub-station at Brearley which, coincidentally, had another 'Death Trap' - the Brearley Bends.

Above right: The final extension to the Halifax tramway system was a very modest one - just a few hundred yards in 1925 to a terminus near the Standard of Freedom at Skircoat Green. Anyone who knows their Halifax will recognise the locality instantly, even the shelter on the left, which still exists today. The tram for Pellon carries an advertisement for 'Wireless', which represented the communications revolution of these inter-war years, bringing a whole world of information and entertainment into people's homes. Skircoat had become an exclusive residential suburb for the 'upwardly mobile' of Halifax in the nineteenth century, and houses that can only be described as mansions were built. Louis John Crossley, for example, of the Dean Clough carpet dynasty, had a fully equipped laboratory and workshop in his Moorside home, and a tramway system in the grounds. Ironically, however, there was no escape, even at Skircoat, from the factory smoke that was creating the wealth to build the mansions. Edward Crossley, cousin of Louis John, had constructed an observatory in the grounds of his house, Bermerside, but was 'discommoded' by the smoke in the atmosphere, which made his giant reflective telescope useless. Henry Savile surrendered his manorial rights at Skircoat Moor (land valued at £40,000) to the Corporation for a nominal £100, one condition being that it tried to abate the 'smoke nuisance'.

Below: The scene is a familiar one in some respects - the junction of George Square and Commercial Street with the public toilets close at hand - but much else that is unfamiliar is revealed in a snapshot of around 65 years ago. Commercial Street then was one of the hubs of the tram system, with vehicles leaving here for many destinations. The Pellon tram stop is clearly visible, as is the one for West End and Highroad Well. The tram tracks heading off towards the bottom left-hand corner would have run up a narrow George Street as compared with today. In fact the track was disused, in anticipation of a redevelopment of George Street that had been mooted in the 1920s, but was not to get underway until the late 1930s. As for the shops, JL White (mantle warehouse) and George Gledhill (hosier) occupied the sites that currently house Specsavers and Klick Photopoint. The tram obscures a frontage that has traditionally been associated with banks, whilst the Prudential sign makes a bold showing on the upper half of Arcade Buildings. Further to the right along Commercial Street, just out of camera shot, was a long-established business that will fall within the memory of many readers - that of Nicholl, Brown & Coyle, sports outfitters.

Bottom: A vehicle that would certainly draw a few appreciative glances in a vintage rally today is the wagon carrying the overhead line maintenance equipment to the right. Adjustments and repairs were often needed, and so the overhead line team had a busy life until trams finally departed the Halifax scene in 1939. Commercial Street in the 1930s, looking towards the dome of what was the National Provincial Bank, gives plenty of evidence as to why it merited that name. As today, large financial institutions intermingling with shops and offices provided the fabric of commerce. The large pair of spectacles on the left was frequently used to advertise the premises of an optician, in this case Sawdons. Either this was a 'throwback' to the Middle Ages, when large trade signs were used to guide an illiterate populace, or it was felt that people in need of an optician needed special help to find one! This left-hand side, between George Square and Silver Street, contained a surprising number of small commercial premises then as compared with now. The only remaining link is the old Midland Bank that was there, now the HSBC. Speaking of large-scale advertising, a visit to Sawdons would certainly have been advisable for anyone missing the huge advertisement for Army Club cigarettes on the gable end.

The sight of a tram, whether in a museum or on a photograph, often induces an incurable bout of nostalgia on the part of some - perhaps an old memory associated with the whine of the motor or the rattle and roll of the motion. Even the greatest tram fans would have to admit, however, that they had their

drawbacks. One of these is illustrated in this shot of Commercial Street, Halifax, as a strange looking vehicle on the left appears to be careering towards the queue of people waiting to board the tramcar. Such dangers were inevitable, of course, with tracks centrally positioned in the road. Those, too, who have ever found themselves

skidding wildly across wet tram tracks, whilst aboard a bicycle or motor-bike, will have experienced the less romantic side of trams. Nevertheless, one thing that can be said is that they did not pollute the atmosphere, which must have helped these people enjoy a sunny day on Commercial Street all the more. At the time of the photograph, the 1930s, there was pollution enough in the air from Halifax's forest of factory chimneys, with houses too making their contribution. The busy scene shows the shop of George Gledhill, hosier and hatter, on the corner of Cheapside, and the rather fine Arcade Buildings to the right, approaching Old Cock Yard.

ote Hill provided quite a challenge to motorists in the tram age. Not only was there a sharp bend, but at this point double tram lines were reduced to a single track. The perils to motorists were clearly stated on the sign above the workmen - 'Motorists. Danger; do not pass trams. No room'. Perhaps the workmen were in the process of widening the road and straightening out the bend a little. The background shows the pleasant fields and copses stretching away towards Warley, and the tower of the parish church, Warley St John's, is just off the picture to the right. Many readers will be familiar with the Peacock Inn, which now occupies the substantial building towards the left of the photograph. Less familiar is the name of the Rose and Crown, a Ramsden's house which can be seen behind the tail of the wagon. The pub was closed during the war and later demolished. Also in this vicinity was the Cote Hill Bobbin Mill, run by the Hirst family for five generations. Established in 1798, the mill produced tens of millions of bobbins for the textile industry. Sadly, the mill could not resist the decline of the industry, and it was forced to close in 1982. Houses with names such as 'The Bobbins', standing on the site of the old mill, provide a faint link with the past.

Below: King Cross is an area which has changed dramatically in relatively recent times although this view, with the church spire in the background, is instantly recognisable even though the photograph dates from the 1930s. The transformation that obliterated large sections of King Cross elsewhere began in the 1960s, with the demolition of houses to the rear of Skircoat Moor Road leading up to Spring Edge. The road was widened and a new fire station was built on the site. Still, it was possible to have a good night out in King Cross in the early 1960s at three of its most notable venues. A start could be made at the Palladium Cinema, and old devotees of this establishment will be interested to know that at its opening, in 1914, it was described as 'more akin to a Jacobean mansion', and possessing red plush seats 'of the tip-up variety'. The next port of call would be for drinks at that fine pub, the Old King, and the evening would not be complete without fish and chips at Wendy's. Both the Old King and Wendy's were swept away, along with much else, in the 1970s road improvement scheme which created the King Cross by-pass in the shape of Aachen Way. As for the Palladium, it closed in 1962 and is now a carpet warehouse.

Bottom: It looks almost like a 'white out' on Commercial Street as a car gingerly noses its way forward around a pair of trams. From the bottom of George Street the domed shape of what is now the National Westminster Bank looms dimly in the distance. Surprisingly, perhaps, the steel wheel on the steel rail of trams provided a good grip in snowy weather, which gave one advantage over buses. In other respects, however, buses were more versatile, and by the 1930s they were making great inroads into the business of the trams. The pictured scene shows every sign of belonging to a weekend blizzard in 1933 which brought havoc to the district. Drifts of six feet were recorded even in the central areas, whilst they reached ten feet in the outlying parts. There was much doubt as to whether Princess Mary would be able to fulfil her official engagements in Halifax that weekend - the opening of two new wards at the Royal Halifax Infirmary and a new carpet-making machine at the Crossley's enterprise at Dean Clough. However the Princess battled her way through from Harewood House, travelling for the most part by train. Meanwhile 700 men with shovels were trying to clear the local roads, shifting an estimated 5000 tons of snow per day over the weekend.

Right until the closure of the Sowerby Bridge route in 1938, the unfortunate residents of this area had to contend with outdated open-top trams. There was a good reason for this, and one which this 1930s photograph illustrates very well. The low railway arch at Sowerby Bridge made it unfeasible to have roofed trams on this route, but perhaps this was scant consolation to those who were forced to brave the wind and the rain. However, these circumstances provided a very compelling reason for the Halifax Building Society to mount a very eye-catching advertisement on the bridge - an invitation to have some sort of roof over your head! The origins of what was to become the biggest building

society in the world lay in a meeting in the Oak Room of the Old Cock Hotel, Halifax, in 1852. Here the founders set up the Halifax Permanent Benefit Building Society, its first headquarters being a shop in the Old Market, rented for £10 per year. Progress was so rapid that even by 1913 the title of the 'biggest' could be claimed, and when a merger came in 1928 with the second largest, the Halifax Equitable, then the position of the new Halifax Permanent Building Society was unchallenged. Change and more change has been the story since then, perhaps the most notable being the transfer of the headquarters from Commercial Street to the new building at Trinity Road in 1973, and the Society's flotation as a bank in 1997.

Wigzell, whose widespread experience had included working in Russia. Building huge steam engines became the firm's speciality, producing more than 1000 in its lifetime, and employing about 400 men at its height. Sadly by 1930 Pollit and Wigzell had fallen victim to the rise of electricity as a source of power and, even more significantly for the locality, the decline of the textile industry.

Top: Traffic congestion we usually regard as a modern phenomenon, but this scene along Fountain Street in 1927 contains all the ingredients for a raising of the temperature on the part of the motorists. Whilst the car on the left seems to be wedged in behind the

Above: Trams were ever prone to rattling and swaying, a characteristic that was made more pronounced by the narrow gauge of the local system. Hence the passengers may well have been enduring a rough ride as this tram swings around the bend and forges along Town Hall Street, Sowerby Bridge, bound for Halifax. Perhaps it was no coincidence that these vehicles sometimes carried advertisements for Typhoo Tea - as a cure for indigestion! The Sowerby Bridge of the 1930s, as shown in the photograph, was an industrial town very much in the local pattern - a mixture of textiles and engineering as the staples. Mills and factories were still largely reliant on steam power, but one important event in 1930 gave a glimpse into the future. The Sowerby Bridge firm of Pollit and Wigzell, with a world-wide reputation for the manufacture of steam engines, closed down. The business had been set up in 1786 at Bank Foundry and the founder's grandson, Joseph Pollit, bought the company in 1862. He was soon joined by Eustace

Triangle tram, the other tram effectively blocks the middle of the road. Most frustrating of all for cars coming from the other direction, the overhead line workers seem to be doing nothing in particular whilst their vehicle nicely takes up that side of the road. And if you thought that all trams looked much the same, the Triangle one demonstrates the open-top, low roof look, vital for the safe negotiation of the low railway arch at Sowerby Bridge. The destination of the middle tram - Old Station - raises the question as to just how many stations Halifax had in 1927. The High Level line terminating at St Paul's had been closed to passengers since 1917, but North Bridge Station was not to close until 1955. Halifax Old was the name given to the present station in 1890 to distinguish it from St Paul's. Originally opened in 1855 to replace a temporary wooden structure at the bottom of Horton Street, and expanded in the 1880s, it was also to be called Halifax Town from 1951, and just plain Halifax from 1961.

Above: Nostalgia 1939 style as representatives of 'transport past' and 'transport future' stand side by side. Trams took their final bow in Halifax on February 14th 1939, after 41 years of coping with one of the country's hilliest systems and carrying 820 million passengers over 75 million miles. The 'test run' of the first electric tram, in May 1898, was for the benefit of the Tramways Committee, with parts of the floor removed so that the motors could be observed. A public service began in June, initially to Highroad Well, but trams proved to be so popular that the network spread almost all over the borough. However, from the mid-1920s the more versatile and economic motor bus began to offer serious competition, and whereas the tram service lost £23,434 in 1927, the buses returned steady profits. Hence the tram system began steadily to contract in the 1930s as buses began to take over. The last trams were given a great send-off on February 14th 1939. At 11pm eight trams set off in convoy from Ovenden to their Halifax depot, and thousands lined the streets on a cold night to bid them farewell. As the photograph shows, the depot had been decorated in their honour. Two of the old trams were still to provide public service, having been converted to a summer house at the Norland Children's Holiday Home.

Above right: A nostalgic as well as a stirring sight, as a powerful engine blows off steam at Halifax Station in 1967. To get the full experience, however, you would need sound effects and the distinctive smell - as well as a bit of soot in your eye! Jubilee Class no 45595, 'Kolhapur', was about to depart with an Easter Monday excursion to Blackpool, with the end of the steam age just one year ahead. Diesels were taking over, cleaner and more economic to run, but lifeless alongside steam engines. To the impatience of Halifax industrialists, there had been some delay before the town was able to join in with the beginnings of the steam age. The railway line along the Calder Valley had opened in 1840, but it was 1844 before a branch line managed to link up Elland with Shaw Syke Station at Halifax. By 1852 a more direct link was created via the very fine 23 arch viaduct at Copley, and thence to Milner Royd, near Sowerby Bridge. Halifax Station was moved rather nearer to its present site and a proper structure was opened in 1855. The rather blackened building to the left of the engine was the expanded and improved version of 1885. The present station is confined to the platform to the right, with just two lines serving it.

round 200 rail enthusiasts arrived at the old St Paul's station, at the junction of Queen's Road and Parkinson Lane, on September 6th 1953. Here they are lovingly clustered around tank engine no 69430, and no doubt a mile or two of camera film was used up that day. The station itself had been closed to passenger traffic in 1917, remaining open as a goods depot until June 1960. Even after 1917, however, joint Mackintosh and Crossley works outings to the seaside set off from St Paul's, and sometimes a circus train arrived there. St Paul's was once the terminus station of the Halifax High Level Railway which joined the Halifax to Queensbury line (opened in 1879) at Holmfield. The construction of the High Level line between 1888 and 1890 was an impressive piece of engineering on the part of the Great Northern Railway Company. Deep cuttings and a tunnel were required, and a ten-arch viaduct carried the line across the Hebble Valley to Wheatley - still there today. Twelve passenger trains each way ran at weekdays, in the first years, and there was a station at Pellon also. Coal comprised much of the goods traffic, but there were also cattle pens at Pellon. The last goods train ran to St Paul's in 1960, and the station was demolished in 1963.

Both pictures: A glamorous visitor, at least in railway terms, arrived at Sowerby Bridge in 1961. The Northern Rubber Company's annual outing from Retford to Blackpool Illuminations was pulled that year by a world record holder, A4 Pacific no 60022, 'Mallard'. It was stopping off at Sowerby Bridge to take on water, and these two photographs show the excitement that had been aroused by the prospect of seeing such an illustrious locomotive. The first shot *(left)* shows 'Mallard' easing its way into Sowerby Bridge Station, with the cameras already clicking. No doubt the local chemists showed a healthy profit that week, processing all the miles of film that were handed in. The second photograph *(below)* finds 'Mallard' briefly at rest, taking into its tender the huge amounts of water that such an engine needed. The enthusiasts, young and old, have gathered round in force, examining every detail, and probably savouring the distinctive smell of a steam locomotive - that acrid mixture of smoke , steam and oil. 'Mallard' was perhaps not the most famous of British locomotives, probably this accolade lay with the 'Flying Scotsman', but the little plaque on its side recorded its claim to fame. In 1938, near Peterborough, it attained the never to be broken world speed record for steam engines of 126 miles per hour, and surely no class of engines had such graceful lines as these streamlined Gresley Pacifics. The excitement at Sowerby Bridge was also due to the fact that such engines usually plied their trade on the London to Scotland east coast express route - a rare sight indeed in the Calder Valley. The scenes around 'Mallard' look a bit hair-raising from the safety point of view, although nothing compared with the chaos of 121 years earlier, when this section of line had been officially opened. The first train to leave Sowerby Bridge, in October 1840, was so packed that people simply stood on top of the carriages, ducking and cheering as they went through tunnels! It has to be said the girl in the foreground does not seem to be part of the worshipping throng. Probably the sight and sound of the green giant impressed her at first, but as talk got around to such matters as tractive effort, boiler pressure per square inch and coal consumption per mile, she became a little distracted. This special train had an observation carriage at the rear, with backward facing seats, allowing panoramic views. Wainhouse Tower stands out so clearly that the observers were bound to be curious about a chimney that was not really a chimney, and one that measured 253 feet at one side, and because of the slope, 285 feet at the other.

Beacon Hill, to the right, frowns down on what still was very much an industrialised Halifax in 1963. So much so that 'Wakes Weeks', the summer holiday fortnight, could be regarded as a time when the town might be 'dead'. This period traditionally fell in early July; the mills closed down; people took their holidays. With many mills closed down permanently, things are a little more flexible now. The train about to move out of the station, hauled by Stanier Class no 42964, was a holiday special to Llandudno, packed with Halifax folk hoping to find some sunshine and fun at the seaside. And what a grimy looking Halifax these holidaymakers were leaving behind, to which the smoke from the engine was liberally contributing. Clean Air Acts had begun in 1956, but the great clean-ups of stonework lay ahead. What surprises people were to find as a result of the sandblasting. For example, the blackened station building to the left, first opened in 1855 but expanded in 1885, has been transformed by cleaning and renovation into the wonderfully stylish structure that we see today. Disused as a station since 1971, much credit goes to Eureka Children's Museum for recognising the building's importance and including it in its plans.

Making a living

I t may look like a Halifax bomb site, but this devastated area of land marks one of the town's earliest twentieth century clearance schemes. Closely packed housing had once filled this area bounded by Orange Street, St James's Road, Great Albion Street and the upper part of modern Broad Street. Known as the Crossfield quarter, but more familiarly dubbed the 'City', it contained 780 people, including 207 children, most of them living in insanitary conditions. The scourge of tuberculosis was more rife in the 'City' than in any other part of town. The decision to demolish went ahead after a two day public

enquiry, and the work began in 1926. The site remained empty for a number of years, but in July 1937 work began on a new cinema. The Odeon arose from the ashes of the 'City', opening in 1938 with a seating capacity of 2050. Later still, in 1954, the Crossfield bus station took up the rest of the site - very handy for the Odeon! Change is constant of course. Many of the buildings in the photograph were to disappear later, including the Alhambra Theatre. The Odeon ceased its life as a cinema in 1975, reopening shortly afterwards as a bingo club. Later still, the bus station migrated from Crossfield to Northgate.

A legacy of learning

Anyone who has travelled up the Ryburn Valley past Ripponden on their way to Oldham or to Junction 22 on the M62 will have passed by the magnificent buildings on the right hand side of the road which house Rishworth School.

Rishworth School was founded by John Wheelwright.

John Wheelwright was professionally a collector of salt duties, although his income seems to have been far larger than that occupation would suggest; he had a flair for business, accumulating property over much of the length of the Calder Valley. A farm at Slitheroe near Rishworth had been acquired by him in 1700, where the now long gone Rishworth railway station would one day be sited, as well as land at Dyson Lane and Clay House at Greetland.

Wheelwright died a wealthy man in 1724 and is buried in Wakefield. Having no near relatives and being of a benevolent disposition John Wheelwright left money in his will to build schools in both Dewsbury and Rishworth. £150 was to come from his estate to build the school in Rishworth and the

annual sum of £10 allocated to pay a schoolmaster for the teaching of 20 boys and girls to be chosen by the trustees from amongst the poorest tenants' children living on any of his estates, whilst any spare places should be allocated to other poor of the parish in which the school stood. According to Wheelwright's will the curriculum should be reading, writing - and such Latin as the trustees might judge to be within pupils capacity to learn. Although co-educational in the spirit of the times and according to Wheelwright's will, of the twenty pupils there should also always be more boys than girls selected for an education.

The pupils were to be lodged at Goathouse under the control of two masters and a 'a sober, discreet and careful woman' to be employed in 'dressing of victuals, washing, bedmaking and other things necessary to looking after the boys and girls' at a sum of £10 per annum.

Money was also set aside in the founder's will for providing funds to allow the best pupils to be sent for further education at Oxford or Cambridge and

Above: *A copy of the school rules from the late 19th century.*
Right: *A game of cricket in the early 1900s.* ***Below:*** *Pupils and staff pictured in 1937.*

gone days, school work began at 7.30 in the morning during the winter months and half an hour earlier during the summer. Even odder, no seats were provided for pupils until 1728 and no forks until 1735!

By 1826 there were 15 girls and 25 boys in the preparatory school and a Grammar school with 30 pupils. Typically of the period girls were required to leave the school at the age of 13, although boys could stay on until the age of 16, or beyond if preparing for university.

New trustees had been elected in 1826 and it was they who drew up plans for a new building for the school. The new school, occupying the present site, was built at a cost of £6,367 on land which was part of the Wheelwright estate, the foundation stone being laid on 14th May 1827 and the new school

towards the cost of the furnishing of Goathouse. Following John Wheelwright's death the new school was completed during 1725. Goathouse or 'Old school' would continue to be used as the school building for over a century.

Today's pupils would undoubtedly find the original school regime a strange one: no-one who could converse in Latin was permitted to speak in any other language whilst the punishment for any infraction of the school rules included not only the possibility of having the left palm hit with a ruler but also potentially the application of the birch to the buttocks - the birch reportedly being known to the pupils, none too affectionately, as 'Black Bill'.

Present day pupils too might quail at the thought that, in those far

Top left: Pupils drilling in 1936.
Above: Staff and pupils pictured in 1928. *Right:* The school in 1932 with Ryburn Dam in the background.

opened in 1828 in what is now the 'Old Building'.

The original school building, Goathouse, would be used first as a joiner's shop until 1839, then as a chapel for the people of Rishworth until 1922, following which it was used as a chapel exclusively by the School once more.

Expansion in pupil numbers inevitably followed the building of the new school. An increase was helped by a decision in 1829 to give tenants on the estate the

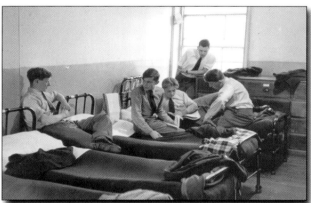

right to nominate children for education at the school. By the following year there were 21 boys in the senior school and 29 in the preparatory school and seven girls. Perhaps as a sign of changing fashions or perhaps an indication of the different standards which emerged following the earlier decision to allow tenants to nominate pupils the following year scholars were barred from wearing clogs for school.

Changing entry requirements did however make some difference: by 1841 pupil numbers had risen to 60 and two years later 70.

In the mid 19th century school inspectors were able to describe Rishworth as the richest educational foundation in Yorkshire with excellent premises,

Top: A lesson in the late 1950s. **Above:** *One of the boys dormitories in 1955.* **Right:** *The Goathouse Chapel.*

a serious and orderly manner amongst pupils and staff and a thoroughness in all its elementary work; military drill drew particular praise.

There is evidence that the school had acquired playing fields by the middle years of the 19th century for playing both football and cricket. The boys in fact played rugger until about 1896 when there was a switch to soccer which would remain the school's main sport until 1928 when it would switch back to rugger. Prior to 1922 the school colours had been blue and white with caps bearing a small metal badge with the Wheelwright coat of arms. The switch to the current maroon and French grey occurred in 1922 coinciding with several other major changes following the retirement of the school's longest serving headmaster.

In 1878 the school appointed the Rev RH Elliott as headmaster; he would become the school's longest

to Rishworth there had been considerable delay in laying cable to the school and as result the school had to use its own one horse power generator until it could be linked to the mains supply.

Nor was electricity the only utility to be of interest to the school. The water supply, for example, from 1827 until 1895 saw water piped from the area of Upper Cockcroft to a cistern in the field below Goathouse. In 1896 £650 was spent improving the supply by improving the Upper Cockcroft reservoir drawing further water from Pike End and creating a new larger cistern near the Goathouse. Maintaining water supplies in those days was important and the school porter had the daily duties of checking the water supply each morning and evening, turning off the stopcocks in addition to lighting fires in the classrooms and cleaning pupils' and masters' shoes each day.

serving head, not retiring until 1919 at the age of 87 after an astonishing 41 years at the helm. They had been difficult years. Pupil numbers had, by the time of Elliott's' retirement, fallen to just 30, of whom only two were girls. These last two left the school in 1921. The school would not become co-educational again until 1968.

It was in the 1920s that the present school uniform made its appearance replacing the Eton collars and mortar boards - and straw boaters worn in the summer - which had been a feature of the school for a century.

By 1923, with a new head, pupil numbers had risen to 65 having doubled within a year. It would however take many years before numbers would grow much larger - on the outbreak of the second world war for example in 1939 there were still a mere 95 pupils rising to 144 by the war's end in 1945 and to over 200 by 1957.

Major new additions to the school buildings have occurred throughout the 20th century. The first of these was a new block completed in 1933 to the north of the old school. In 1950 Heathfield, the former residence of JH Wheelwright, a former chairman of the governors, was acquired for use as a preparatory school, since when a variety of additions have been made to the building. Four years later Slitheroe House

Those 200 scholars in the 1950s would find certain aspects of the school not too dissimilar to today: oil lamps, gas mantles and candles for example had long since disappeared. During the Christmas holidays in 1927 electric lighting was installed replacing gas lighting which had been used for illumination since the 1860s. When electricity had come

Top: The swimming pool at Heathfield.
Right: An early photograph of pupils and staff.

was taken over to provide accommodation for a junior entry of 11 year olds.

In 1957 a new block of buildings was erected on the bottom field to provide a lecture room three class-rooms and a small laboratory. Two years later the Chan music school was opened, named after a parent who had contributed largely to the cost. Perhaps one of the most valued additions however was the swimming pool built in the mill behind Heathfield and named after Fred Bentley.

Many more changes both small and large have since occurred. Each generation of pupils returning after a few years to their old school would see something of significance which had not been there in their day. Quite often those old pupils would have made signif-icant contributions to those improvements.

The Old Rishworthian Club is closely associated with the school and at the start of the 21st century had around 800 ex-pupils as members, some whom had been pupils as long ago as the 1920s. The Club holds two formal reunions each year. Under the terms of a deed of trust dating from 1954 the OR Club supports a schol-arship fund which provides bursaries or scholarships for the sons and daughters of former pupils at the discretion of the Board of Trustees in agreement with the headmaster and School Governors.

Left: The netball team braving the icy Pennine conditions in 1968. Below: The orchestra rehearsing in the school hall, now the library.

Today Rishworth is a thriving independent school with a happy mix of day-pupils and weekly and full boarders. The school is an exceptionally friendly, caring community in which pupils are as strongly encouraged to rejoice in each other's achievements as to take pride in their own.

The school has its own Junior School, Heathfield, and offers a continuous educational provision to boys and girls from the age of three to eighteen.

Pupils generally relish their time at Rishworth giving of their best, finding the work rewarding, forging lasting friendships, enjoying excellent relations with their teachers and developing an enduring loyalty to the school.

Rishworth's magnificent buildings, extensive grounds and superb location provide pupils with a physical environment which is conducive both to the clarity of mind

love of learning and the will to succeed, a sense of responsibility, self discipline, purpose and fulfilment together with an appreciation of personal virtues and spiritual values such as honesty, dependability, perseverance, commitment, humility and respect for others.

When the time comes for pupils to leave the school the staff and governors hope the school has helped them not only to be fully prepared for the next stage in their lives but also to be the confident balanced and considerate young men and women society would like all youngsters to be.

In 2024 Rishworth School will celebrate its three hundredth anniversary. That anniversary will provide a unique opportunity to reflect on the remarkable legacy of John Wheelwright. That legacy has not been just the school buildings but more importantly it has also been the generation upon generation of pupils who have passed through the school gates to leave Rishworth as young men and women, who are not only equipped to help shape the future but also have an understanding of the past.

required for study and to the full and balanced development of young people. Facilities are excellent and include a spacious sports hall, a 25 metre indoor swimming pool, a large expanse of games pitches, a recently refurbished music block, modern IT suites, a new performing arts theatre and a new Sixth Form Centre.

The unusually high degree of individual attention afforded to pupils by small teaching groups, the careful monitoring of progress, co-ordinated pastoral support and a close working partnership with parents enables pupils to build on their strengths and allows individual needs to be addressed.

Taught by a qualified staff of dedicated specialists the curriculum, both academic and non academic, is broad and stimulating offering every pupil the chance to be challenged and to excel. Justly Rishworth enjoys a high reputation in sport, music, art and drama. During pupils' time at Rishworth the school tries to ensure that in addition to the knowledge and skills acquired through academic study they develop a

Top: *The school as it is at the start of a new millennium.*
Above left: *The school gymnastic club in 1991.*
Left: *One of the new pupils at Heathfield Preparatory School.*
Right: *Richard Baker, the school's current headmaster.*

From one horse-power to diesel power

Calderdale has a number of well known haulage firms operating within its boundaries, few however have been in existence since the first world war - and fewer still have remained in the same family since that time. But one at least can make such a claim to fame.

The Halifax haulage and fuel delivery business of W Greenwood & Sons was founded in 1916 by the sixteen year old Walter Greenwood. Walter's father, Tom Greenwood, was a horse driver in Holmfield and was a major encouragement to his son.

The haulage company is still run solely by the Greenwood family: today the fourth generation of the Greenwood family is taking the firm into the new millennium.

Due to bad eyesight, which prevented him joining the forces during the first world war, young Walter instead bought a donkey and an old cart, using money he had saved from selling eggs from hens which he kept, and began his own business. At the time Walter also had a full time job working in a local foundry lifting heavy shell cases for the women who were employed there on war work, but Walter wanted to work for himself. It was not long before Walter swapped his donkey for a horse and the business began to grow.

Right: *The young Walter and Doris in 1926.*
Below: *Young Walter, second from left, with his family.*

Walter Greenwood, the youngest of six children, was still living at home with his parents in a house next to the Bethel Methodist Church in Ovenden. His horse and cart were kept in a small triangular field at Near Royd Farm, Ovenden; he eventually gained a licence to deliver goods within a 15 mile radius of Ovenden post office. His first job however was collecting meat from the abattoir in Halifax to deliver to local butchers.

Once when returning home from a job in Sowerby, and with night drawing on, Walter was stopped by a policeman in Sowerby Bridge for not showing any lights. The policeman helped Walter light the lamps

and sent him on his way. When he arrived home late he expected his mother to be angry or at least anxious - or both, but she was neither: the Sowerby Bridge policeman had telephoned a colleague at Ovenden police station and asked him to let Walter's mother know he was running late. Those were the days!

In 1924 Walter married his wife, Doris; they would work together for many years, she patiently helped with the horses and carts, harnessing the horses and polishing their brasses, especially for galas and Whit Sundays. The Greenwoods had two children Margaret and William Arthur. William Arthur was destined to become the second generation to work in the business, and on leaving school drove a horse and cart alongside his father.

When one of Walter Greenwood's friends, Dick Halliday, became ill he bought a fuel delivery round from him and the business grew a little more. Walter delivered coal to all the local households in Ovenden. It was hard work: a generation has now grown up which has never seen the coalman delivering sacks of coal with a horse and cart but many readers will still remember seeing the coal-blackened delivery men heaving sacks of coal from their carts or lorries to be tipped down the shutes to our cellars or into coal sheds. Heaving a full sack of coal onto one's shoulder always seemed an almost impossible feat, but coalmen seemed to be able to undertake that awesome task with ease.

During the second world war rationing meant there was a limited amount of coal to deliver but Walter was able to secure work from local firms delivering pig-iron and other engineering products.

Above left: *The firm's Certificate of Registration, 1958.* ***Left:*** *All harnessed up and ready for business, 1950s.* ***Below:*** *Children dressed up for an outing in 1950s.*

William Arthur Greenwood served in the forces during the second world war, but joined his father at the war's end. By now the business had two horses and carts, one driven by Walter and one by William. Furniture removal was another major job that was run alongside the fuel and general haulage business.

The two Greenwoods, father and son, hauled coal from the railway sidings in Holmfield. The trains only stayed for a short while before they would depart; if they were not emptied before their departure time 'demurrage' was charged per truck. It was a demanding job emptying the trucks quickly to avoid having to pay a financial penalty, then delivering to all the local houses and mills.

Walter Greenwood was not too enthusiastic about motor lorries; he said he trusted his horses which knew where the customers were on the rounds and needed little effort to complete their rounds - unlike the modern alternative. William Arthur Greenwood however was keen to progress from horses to motorised vehicles and finally, in 1949, he persuaded his father to buy their first vehicle. The number AJX 955 is long remembered in the Greenwood family. The Bedford tipper was bought from Dews Garage for £490. The business developed once more with the introduction of the motorised vehicle, the two men running the fuel and the haulage alongside one another.

Rubbish and ashes were moved from mills such as Calverts mills at Club Lane and at Illingworth, Moorley's Mill at Beechwood Road, Gee's Dye House at Shay Lane and J Ludlow at Ovenden. Deliveries were also undertaken from those mills.

In December 1946 William Greenwood had married Edna Garside. Eventually they would have three children: Jennifer, Peter and Rodney. Jennifer chose a career in hairdressing and had a local shop for many years. Peter and Rodney initially both chose careers in joinery but Peter soon changed his mind in 1970 choosing to join his father instead in the haulage business; and Peter was soon followed by Rodney.

By the late 1950s early starts were being made to collect Lion Coal Bricks from the plant at Shaw Cross Colliery in Dewsbury. The company prospered and in

Top right: *William Arthur with his two sons Peter and Rodney.* ***Above right:*** *From left, the young Rodney, Peter, Jane and Linda in 1973.* ***Left:*** *Walter and Doris in their Golden Wedding year, 1974.*

1956 William Arthur Greenwood bought the remaining shares in the still small company from his father. In 1962 William Greenwood bought his second vehicle, this time an Austin tipper with the registration number RCP 144. This vehicle was bought from Thomas Greenwood & Sons of Horton Street and cost £1,226. By now Walter Greenwood had decided to retire and passed the business over completely to his son William.

Between 1962 and 1964 with William at the wheel the new Austin tipper was busy locally helping with demolishing the pre-fabricated housing built during the war in the areas of Foundry Street, Ovenden and Dudley Crescent, Illingworth.

Over the following decade the business continued to grow, not least when W Greenwood & Sons bought out Harry White's small haulage business based in Hopwood Lane. That expansion meant taking on work from Willey Pearson at Scarboro' Mills, King Cross, Asquith's of High Road Well and Churchill Redman's.

During these years the business flourished. In 1972 a new vehicle was purchased for long distance haulage, a Dodge flat bed truck, UKW 386K, at a cost of £2,404.

Business confidence had earlier been badly dented by a council letter to tenants advising them of a changeover to North Sea Gas from their coal fires. This was to effect the coal delivery side of the business badly though the haulage side of the firm continued to grow; indeed it had been in anticipation of the effect of the Clean Air Act that William Greenwood had been reluctant to encourage his two sons to come into the haulage business with him and instead encouraging them to go into joinery though allowing them to work alongside him in the winter months when the construction industry was quiet. The general haulage side of the business had to be developed if the firm was to survive: it was then that the firm of H White (Haulage) of Hopwood Lane was taken over and the family set to work developing its already sound customer base. Fortunately the strategy worked: within the next couple of years the fleet grew to four vehicles, three on general haulage and the fourth on fuel deliveries.

A very eventful year in the Greenwoods'

Top right: *One of Greenwood's vehicles taking part in a gala.* ***Above left:*** *One of the many loads of straw delivered by the firm each year.* ***Left:*** *One of the trucks the firm inherited when they took over Joseph Hartley's business in 1986.*

lives came in 1974, the year in which Walter and Doris celebrated their Golden wedding. It was also the year that Rodney married Linda Holden; they would subsequently have three children Melanie, Kathryn and Thomas. Shortly after being married however Rodney and Linda moved to Near Royd Farm; the farming business ran alongside the haulage and fuel business. The following year Peter Greenwood married Jane Wood, subsequently having two children of their own: Christopher and Amy.

Hay and straw haulage was now part of the business alongside farming; usually about 80 loads were moved each season: all the family joined in to help take the deliveries off. The haulage business however saw a decline in these years and so Peter Greenwood bought Mason Green Farm in 1982 to run alongside Near Royd Farm. Ironically the day Peter and Jane moved in to their farm Peter was called away on an urgent driving trip and the haulage business seemed to increase in leaps from that day onwards.

There was a boom in the building industry just then which saw major changes in demand; investment in 'crane off' vehicles became the order of the day.

William Arthur Greenwood died suddenly in 1980 leaving the family in deep shock; his wife Edna decided to sell the business on to her two sons Peter and Rodney after managing the business herself for a year leaving the third generation of Greenwoods running the firm along with their wives.

By the mid 1980s the firm was running a fleet of eight vehicles and was still growing; by 1990 it had 11 vehicles - and all British built! By now the business was offering a countrywide service. Jane and Linda were now to become full-time workers in the business alongside their husbands.

In March 1985 Walter Greenwood, the firm's founder, passed away, after maintaining a keen interest in the business right up to his death.

By then the business was struggling for space for its vehicles to park and so in 1986 bought the firm of Joseph Hartley coal merchants in Holmfield. A one acre site was included in the purchase which was to become the main business headquarters. The acquisition also uplifted the solid fuel business, with the Greenwoods running Joseph Hartley's vehicle alongside their own.

At the beginning of the 1990s the firm's first articulated vehicle were bought; unfortunately the building boom had slowed down but luckily Greenwoods was now able to acquire work from a local wire firm - the Standard Wire company in Sowerby Bridge where Greenwoods sent five vehicles every day.

Christopher, Melanie, Kathryn and Thomas, representing the fourth generation of the family in the business, have all at some time helped in the firm.

In 1994 Peter's son, Christopher, joined the company as a driver, starting with a four and a half tonner and working his way up to be a class one driver, driving an articulated vehicle; Christopher also helped his father, Peter, with the solid fuel round.

As Rodney's daughters, Melanie and Kathryn, grew they also helped run the solid fuel cash and carry side of the business at weekends, shortly followed by their brother Thomas who still works there at weekends alongside his father.

The solid fuel yard at Holmfield was further developed in 1996 into a haulage depot which

Above: The coal yard. **Left:** *The old tipper truck recently restored by Peter Greenwood.*

would eventually see the development of a three bay maintenance workshop. By now the business had 14 vehicles, all being maintained in-house.

It was two years later, in 1998, that the haulage business of W Greenwood & Sons moved into its new maintenance workshop. Today the business runs a mixed fleet of vehicles: four 'artics', four crane vehicles, four flat vehicles and six 'curtain siders' covering the whole country for its firm customer base.

In recent years Rodney Greenwood has taken the step of recreating the history of the firm by acquiring a cart for one of his shire horses to draw. Peter and Rodney's father, William Arthur Greenwood, started his part of the business off with his Bedford tipper truck: Peter Greenwood has now restored a vehicle from those bygone days.

The business has always supported local charities and both horse and cart and the Bedford truck can be seen at local shows and galas, a happy reminder of the days which sadly recede further and further from our recall.

Today the Greenwood family firm is noted for its reliability, well-liveried vehicles and loyal workforce. What enormous changes the business has seen over the course of almost a century in haulage: certainly the founder Walter Greenwood who would have been 100 years old on 17th November 2000, could never have guessed back in 1916 what his firm would develop into from that modest start with just a single donkey cart.

Top right: *Greenwood's first prizewinning float in the 2000 Halifax Gala.* ***Above:*** *Some of today's modern fleet of vehicles.* ***Left:*** *Greenwood's vehicles at their headquarters.* ***Below:*** *Coming full circle, the recently restored cart from Greenwood's earliest days of trading.*

Transparently excellent

A company with a world class reputation in the production of quality products for the glass industry is now entering its third century of manufacture from its premises in Holmfield, Halifax. Parkinson Spencer Refractories has been a family-run business for seven generations. From 1800 to the present day fireclay, mined from the deposits owned by the firm, has been supplied in one form or another to the glass industry in the United Kingdom and throughout the world.

There is the evidence of considerable mining activity in the immediate vicinity of their works. At one time there were a number of firms in the Halifax area which utilised the clays to be found there, manufacturing firebricks, sanitaryware and clay pipes but the number has declined and PSR is one of only a small number of survivors.

As the glass industry advanced during the course of the Industrial Revolution it gradually became evident that the best quality clay for making refractories was to be found in only two locations. These were at Stourbridge in the (now) West Midlands and at Halifax. Despite the availability of clay and coal in the area there were no glassworks in Halifax as, until the Aire & Calder Navigation had been extended close to Halifax in the late 18th century, followed by the railways fifty years later, the town was remote and inaccessible.

The company's founder Caleb Spencer was born in 1766. He was apprenticed to a local farmer, but later on he was to be found running the Dog & Gun Inn at Oxenhope which had rights to the seam of clay on the neighbouring land. His daughter married David Parkinson, who made his living from coal, clay, stone and the land (he supplied the stone for the building of the Black Dyke Mills in Queensbury). By the middle of the 19th century the interests of the two families were centred more and more on the clay and fire-brick manufacturing business, trading under the name of

Above: *The manufacture of glasshouse pots circa 1940.*
Below: *Grinding refractory blocks circa 1940.*

refractory blocks for glass production which could withstand the increasingly high temperatures demanded by the new furnaces. Stourbridge clay was found to be less resilient than the Halifax clay in these circumstances.

Caleb Parkinson had the enviable ability to identify sources of Halifax Hard Bed Clay and to determine the correct point at which to start extraction so when the shareholders of the Spencer family tried once too often to interfere with the way he and his brother Spencer wanted to run things, they decided to set up another business to buy clay deposits on their own, known as C & S Parkinson. The dispute centred around the expectation that a cousin, Harry Newton would be given paid

Parkinson & Spencer. By the end of the century the seam of clay they had been mining at May Royd was nearing exhaustion so the company moved to Holmfield.

The first world war was a catalyst for change in the industry. The adoption of a more scientific approach to the manufacturing process contributed to a much-needed increase in efficiency and cost-effectiveness. Caleb Parkinson, by now the fourth generation of the original founding family, embraced the challenge of change enthusiastically and set about producing

Top: *Clay mining in Shibden Valley, circa 1930.*
Above: *Hand ramming refractory blocks, circa 1940.*

employment in the firm at a time when the brothers were being denied the cash for capital expenditure - the upshot of all this was the formation of the limited company Parkinson & Spencer Ltd in 1921. But there were many problems ahead, costs including wages, were increasing and production was hit by a series of miners' strikes which affected the firm in two ways as both clay and coal were required to run the business. The 1920s also saw improvements in the way refractory blocks were made and was a time during which new materials were evaluated and incorporated into the production process.

Parkinson & Spencer were typical of the UK refractory industry during the 1920s and 1930s. The firm

adopted methods of ramming, slip-casting and vacuum slip-casting and worked constantly to improve the composition of its clay pots, subjecting them to frequent analysis and adopting the analyst's recommendations. The firm also benefited from the growing realisation that the Halifax clay was superior to the Stourbridge clay. The business also received a substantial boost when a tariff was introduced on imported glass and in 1933 business was very brisk. It was also during this period that the firm started to send its products overseas, to Spain, South Africa, New Zealand, Australia, Greece, Norway, India and Italy, and even Argentina.

The declaration of war in September 1939 was the beginning of a period of great activity and great difficulty for the glass industry. There were many orders but they lost a large number of workers to the forces. The firm also had difficulty complying with black-out regulations since the coal-fired kilns would throw out flames from

the chimneys when they were being stoked up. To disguise the kiln a loose wooden structure was placed every night round the fires and adjacent coal stocks. This created appalling working conditions for the kiln stokers and the temptation to let in some fresh air on a quiet night was very strong. As well as shortage of materials, spare parts, and labour, the industry also came under central state control from August 1941. Scarcity brought rising costs and prices shot up at regular intervals. By the end of 1940, for example, prices were already on average twenty per cent higher than in the last days of peace. The loss of men to the forces brought a lapse in quality as a number of highly experienced men left to join the services. Women were recruited to take the place of men and towards the end of the war the firm took on prisoners of war. By November 1944 prisoners of war accounted for half the firm's labour.

Top: *Loading refractory blocks by hand.*
Above: *The pride of the fleet in the 1950s.*
Left: *Exporting refractory blocks in the 1960s.*

In 1941 the firm made an historic purchase - the Spencer family's interest in the Dog & Gun Inn and the adjoining land at Oxenhope where Caleb Spencer had first begun extracting clay in the early 19th century.

The strain of wartime production took its toll on Spencer Parkinson who was advised by his doctor in March 1945 to take a long rest. His brother, Caleb, suspected he would not return and in fact he retired a month later though he remained a director until his early death in October 1951.

Doris Spencer died around the same time and she was replaced on the board by Harry Newton whose request for a place in the family firm had caused the dissolution of the original firm a quarter of a century before. In the meantime he had acquired experience with a subsidiary of ICI, as the director of a soda ash factory in South Africa, making him the ideal candidate for the Parkinson & Spencer board and he proved a valuable source of advice until his death in 1970.

For a brief period Caleb Parkinson was left to run the business without any managerial assistance. On 3 September 1945 his son, Henry Parkinson joined the firm. Henry had had the benefit of studying under the eminent Professor Turner at Sheffield University from where he graduated in 1943. He spent two years with ICI at Billingham before returning to the family company where his initial concern was to raise production standards. He joined his father and Harry Newton on the board in 1946.

After the end of the second world war the firm was overwhelmed with orders resulting from pent-up demand but there was still a serious shortage of materials. Sillimanite, an important raw material, for example was very scarce until 1949; in the previous year the firm at times had barely enough to operate one day a week. Strikes by Yorkshire miners and the appalling winter of 1947, which created a drain on the country's energy resources, also made the supply of coal erratic. Plans for modernising the firm's buildings and plant were also delayed because they were still subject to the wartime system of licensing and building and other raw materials were in short supply nationally.

Nevertheless, in 1947 after suffering much due to unreliable supplies of coal, the firm was able to switch to oil-fired kilns. This marked the end of an era. Bringing the kilns up to the required temperature, evenly spread throughout the kiln and keeping the temperature constant was a

Above: *Two early brochures.*
Below: *The premises circa 1945.*

consummate art where the use of coal was concerned. Oil-fired kilns by comparison were much easier to operate and the skill of the kiln-stokers was consequently lost.

The company introduced many new working practices during the years immediately following the end of the second world war, a result of Henry Parkinson's two-month study tour of the refractory industry in the Hartford and St Louis, Missouri areas of the United States. By 1954 the firm was making 550 clay pots per year. Pot making was becoming an increasingly rare skill. The process was so closely guarded senior pot makers often refused to carry on working if someone else entered the room. A modern pot-making workshop in which the temperature and humidity were thermostatically controlled to ensure the clay could dry evenly enabled a skilled pot-maker to produce a dozen pots a month. Each pot, holding up to three-quarters of a ton of molten glass was expected to last anything above three months in production. Temperatures of 1350 deg C were now 100 deg C higher than thirty years previ-

ously. A further significant step was taken by the company in 1957 when they decided to replace the old intermittent kilns with a new continuous tunnel kiln; this was cheaper to install and operate than the old type of kilns. The cost was £60,000, and purchased mainly with a preferential loan from the Ministry of Fuel and Power. It was ideally suited to the firm's product range at the time. It took five kiln cars carrying up to five tons of refractory blocks every other day, operating on a three week cycle. It was later converted from oil to natural gas.

The 1960s were prosperous for the firm and saw a considerable expansion of the export business. Henry Parkinson took over as Managing Director in 1960. In addition the company was also seeking ways of expanding its product range, and in-house research and development work was undertaken to improve sillimanite and mullite blocks. A licence agreement made with the Hartford Empire Corporation, known under the Emhart name, opened up the

Above: *Glasshouse pots awaiting despatch.*
Below: *The offices in 1960.*

chance for the company to supply numerous glass-making firms world-wide. As a result, export sales had increased to seventy per cent of total sales by the end of 1985.

David Parkinson, Henry's son, the seventh generation of the family to join the business, came onto the Board of Directors in 1976. At that time it was felt that a change of name from Ambler Thorn Fire Clay Works would be beneficial and the company was named Parkinson-Spencer Refractories Ltd, and later became universally known as PSR.

By the close of the 1980s, exports accounted for 78 per cent of turnover and the company's four main product lines, feeder expendables, furnace blocks, forehearth refractories and glasshouse pots all contributed equally to sales and profits. Computers came to the company in the early 1980s, as well as the realisation of the need to meet internationally recognised quality standards. Many changes to the firm's production techniques were necessary before the company was granted the quality assurance standard of BS5750/ISO9002 in 1993.

The years since 1990 have seen radical changes in PSR's product range as the company has responded to a rapidly changing world market. The use of glasshouse pots for the melting of glass has been gradually superseded by newer technologies, although perversely PSR has been left as the only UK source, and one of the few world sources, for this unique and specialised product.

The most significant change of direction, however, has been the shift into engineered products complimentary to the company's mainstream refractory products. Primarily used in the glass container manufacturing industry, but also to be found in the tableware, lighting and TV glass industries, PSR's forehearth systems combine a knowledge and experience in the manufacture of special refractory shapes with the complex sciences of glass thermal conditioning. This evolution has transformed the company from its traditional fireclay origins into one that is internationally renowned for advanced glass conditioning systems.

The company has prospered by producing quality products and responding to changes by introducing new products and methods. These principles have stood PSR, a world leader in its specialist field, in good stead for over two centuries and will continue to do so in the future.

This page: *The premises today at Holmfield.*

Engineering the difference for half a century

I t is likely that many readers will have bought or consumed a product whose manufacture was aided by the Fan Systems Group, so diverse are the applications of the technology which it has spent the last fifty years exploring and developing.

Fan Systems Ltd was established on 16 March, 1950 by three employees of another fan company, Musgrave Fans. These three, Messrs Murphy, Simkins and Vaudrey based the company in Piccadilly, Manchester and expanded the business rapidly, supplying industrial fans and drying systems to their numerous customers. Mr Murphy was the Managing Director, Mr Vaudrey was involved with the supply of equipment to the glass industry and Mr Simkins took responsibility for supplying fans to the heavy clay industry.

Fan Systems has remained one of the foremost suppliers of fans to the Nuclear industry and took their first orders from the then Atomic Energy Board in 1950. They have been continually and actively involved in the design of systems, working in partnership with nuclear construction engineers to achieve the optimum solutions to meet the stringent demands of the industry.

Owing to the firm's success the Piccadilly site became inadequate and in 1954 it proved necessary to

Both pictures: *Fans ready for despatch in the early 1950s.*

relocate to another Manchester site, this happened again in 1960.

Initially a lot of production was subcontracted to other engineering companies but from 1957 the company started fan production in Slaithwaite, near Huddersfield.

the former Blackpool Railway Station. The Managing Director of PM Walker at the time spotted the dismantling of the station and put in an offer for the structure - the building is still in use today.

Turnover steadied from 1978 onwards and sales strategy became more aggressive and the company started to supply new industries including the paper drying and automotive industry, their clients included such big names as Hyundai and Ford.

In 1963, Fan Systems took over the manufacture of fans for a company called Andrew Weatherfoils and in doing so acquired drawings of new fan designs as well as a number of high profile customers involved in the nuclear industry, who have remained with the company ever since. Other sectors supplied with numerous centrifugal fans were the heavy-clay, ceramic, tobacco and carpet industries (including the famous Dean Clough operation in Halifax).

Expanding further in 1965, Fan Systems took over PM Walker who produced their own fans as well as being involved in air conditioning and sheet metal working.

In 1978, the company moved offices and production to its present site in Greetland, Halifax. The physical framework of the factory was purchased and built from

In the 1980s production and turnover steadied as the company concentrated on the production of specialised centrifugal fans to a number of core businesses. This action enabled the company to survive the recession of the early 1990s but was not expanding as quickly as the Directors would have liked.

The solution came in 1993 when the Witt Group, one of the world leaders in fan manufacture recognised the untapped potential in Fan Systems and acquired the company. Witt & Son was established in the late 1940s

Top: *A consignment of fans leaving for a Scottish microchip manufacturer.* ***Above left:*** *Fan destined for a former Halifax brick works.* ***Above:*** *Direct driven centrifugal fan for a soap manufacturer in Lancashire.*

as a specialised manufacturer of fans to the German merchant shipbuilding industry. Their well-proven expertise in axial and centrifugal fan manufacture has made them market leaders in many specialised high performance sectors. It is no idle boast that Witt fans are used on in excess of 12,000 ships globally - this figure represents approximately 10 per cent of the current world-wide fleet. Witt introduced an unparalleled level of technology to the company and Fan Systems had access to a wider range of fans which they had never previously been able to supply. The company's range of fans complemented each other well and by 1999, turnover had grown to a figure in excess of £3 million.

Drawing on Witt's reputation and expertise Fan Systems was able to enter the UK shipbuilding industry via the MOD for the UK Navy. This had been a previously impossible and closed market. In addition this led to the opening up of export markets in Scandinavia, Middle East and even South America, in addition to the existing North America and Pacific Rim markets. Fan Systems Group now produces one of

the largest ranges of industrial fans in the UK. Their fans are used in a wide variety of industries including nuclear, process, marine, furnace and glass sectors, both in the UK and overseas.

The extensive Witt range of fans and their design programme were integrated into Fan Systems' expanded CAD facilities. This now enables Fan Systems to give a rapid turnaround, typically within 48 hours, for quotations and all support documentation. They also offer fan specifications on disk to enable customers to make their own fan selection and noise calculations.

Top: *A selection of V Belt Driven fans for the tobacco industry (1980s).* **Above:** *An oxidiser plant in Derbyshire where the firm's fans are installed (1990s).* **Left:** *Two size 48 NA Type Fans with Energy Storing Flywheel Drives (1970s), for use with a Thermal Chemical Plant Oxidiser Installation in Scotland.*

and Management departments Martin Downs and director, Ernst Wehden have each spent 35 years in the fan industry.

In every industrial process there are areas where specialised air movement or air treatment can be employed to increase productivity or profitability. Within these areas Fan Systems are able to undertake initial investigations, make recommendations and where these are accepted, to design, fabricate and install complete systems. Some areas in which the company has worked are drying (particularly heavy clays), recovery of residual heat and its redeployment, swarf collection, air pollution control, dust extraction, fume extraction, noise and vibration isolation as well as tunnel ventilation.

Recently there has been a major effort to increase the volume of e-commerce based trading and the company has launched its own web-site. They have also produced the industry's first CD Business Card, on which there is the company's entire product catalogue, service catalogue, operating and maintenance manual in seven languages, along with a company profile all on a CD the size of a credit card.

Underlining both Fan Systems' and Witt philosophy is a commitment to total quality, Witt procedures have been certified to comply with the German nuclear and marine quality standards and they were one of the first companies to achieve accreditation to ISO 9001 TÜV. There are presently 40 on-site staff and also a specialised acoustics department and a well established Service and Maintenance Division. Every fan manufactured is test run and quality recorded to ensure the customer is entirely satisfied with the quality and performance of the fans they produce and supply. Fan Systems are a progressive company and believe in continually striving to improve the products they offer. The research and development budget is on average five per cent of the annual company turnover.

Fan Systems firmly believe that their commitment to the customer does not end with the supply of the fan to site. Records have been kept for every fan manufactured in over fifty years of the company's history. A network of engineers across the country has been established to offer advice and provide after sales service to ensure that all customer expectations are met.

The firm has always been an excellent employer, providing employees with a good working environment and in return many of its staff have remained loyal to the company. John Barry Garner and Abe Manning will have both worked in the factory for 40 years in 2001, whilst Tony Mitchell has worked there for 30 years. In the Sales

Fan Systems turnover has grown by 270 per cent since 1997 and this is reflected in the plans to further expand and develop its current Greetland site. With this expansion, Fan Systems, with a projected turnover in excess of £4 million (in 2001), will be well on course to proceed with their objective of making the company the predominant UK specialist manufacturer of industrial fans.

Top left: *Fan Systems are heavily involved in the Nuclear Industry.* *Top right:* *Long-time employees, Abe Manning, Tony Mitchell and John Barry Garner.* ***Above left:*** *Jet fans installed in a German tunnel.* ***Right:*** *The launch of Wave Knight, with centrifugal fans provided by Fan Systems, 2000.*

Delving them hills

One thing which sets us apart from 'them over the hill' in Lancashire is the relative absence of brick. Stone, good Yorkshire stone, is what sets us apart. The Ripponden firm of O&W Crawshaw Ltd, a Member of the National Federation of Builders, has contributed much to our stone-built architectural heritage.

O&W Crawshaw became a limited company in 1956 although the business had been in existence for much longer. Brothers, Orlando and William Crawshaw, had worked for their father Johnathan Crawshaw and his brother Richard Arthur Crawshaw who had earlier traded as Crawshaw Bros. Nor were the Crawshaw brothers the only Crawshaws in the local stone masonry business: two of Johnathan and Richard Arthur Crawshaw's older brothers also practised the same trade and a third was an architect to many of the earlier projects. Crawshaw stone masons have been round for generations, the trade having been passed down from father to son.

According to family history the Crawshaw family had originally been Flemish weavers who had entered this country via the Humber in the late 18th century, leaving quite a few relatives still living in the Barton-on-Humber area.

The family were staunch Methodists and were actively involved in the establishment and building of the Stones Methodist Church and School in Ripponden from the earliest years of the 19th century, even before the Battle of Trafalgar in 1805. Weavers, Joseph and John Crawshaw of Round Ing, Rishworth were amongst the first trustees of the Stones Methodist Chapel. Such

Top left: *William Crawshaw.* **Above right:** *Bryan Crawshaw.* **Above far right:** *Johnathan Crawshaw and his wife Alice.* **Right:** *Stones Methodist Chapel.*

support would continue for generations: one of the early burials there records the passing of Joseph Crawshaw's wife who died at the age of 89 years in 1844; her headstone records that she was the mother, grandmother, great grandmother and great great grandmother to an astonishing 397 descendants.

By the mid 19th century the Crawshaw name appears as stone masons in the local gazetteer. Generally however members of the family continued to be weavers, the oldest members having started in the weaving business at the age of only eight in the mill, some leaving to work with stone when they became strong enough for the heavier work required in the building industry. And the work was hard: William Crawshaw could recall having to walk to work in Elland pushing a wheelbarrow all the way from Ripponden, and having to be there for 7.30 am!

Bryan Crawshaw, who would eventually succeed his father and uncle, was in turn followed by his sons Alan and Graham as joint managing directors. Alan served his apprenticeship with the firm whilst Graham was apprenticed to a joiner in Barkisland before working in Salford and Rochdale as a building clerk of works. Graham also spent seven years part time teaching building skills theory at Percival Whitley College before joining his brother Alan following the sudden and premature death of their father, Bryan.

The family at first was only involved in masonry but later made a natural progression to become quarry owners. The present business began in the Ripponden Wood area before moving to Castle Quarry in Nursery Lane, Ripponden early in the 20th century.

During the first world war Orlando Crawshaw had served in the army; his brother William however was able to stay at home and 'mind the shop' a result of an accident with a crane whilst building part of Stones Mill at Ripponden in which he suffered a fractured skull and the loss of one eye. William's absence from service would be made up for in the second world war when his son Bryan would train as a pilot in the RAF.

Top left: Orlando and William working with men at Castle Quarry. *Top right:* Bryan Crawshaw at the opening of the Chan Music School at Rishworth School. *Above:* Work at Cockroft, Rishworth. *Right:* Alan Crawshaw pictured during conversion work at Kershaw House.

In the early days family members worked on the tools as masons doing what little paperwork was required after the day's work was done. Paperwork was simple then, not least because prices were stable, people knew how much they would have to pay a mason without asking and often the Crawshaws were commissioned, do the work and a bill would then follow priced for time and materials. Today most work is carried out on quotation basis, although some jobs are still carried out using the older time and material calculation.

Whilst Castle Quarry has always operated as a builders' yard, until the early 1950s it was also where stone was both quarried and worked. At one time there was a small crane there but usually the stone was brought out using hand levers and rollers and then split up using wedges or 'plugs and feathers'. The site still houses a 25 HP single cylinder Blackstone stationary

yards digging graves, building vaults and installing monumental masonry.

Over the years the firm has changed the face of Calderdale having been involved with building most of the stone built terraced or detached properties visible on the approach to Ripponden. Other projects have included Elland baths in 1900, Victoria Mill, Elland, Barkisland Mill, Boulderclough Chapel, Stones School in Ripponden, Stones Chapel and the old Halifax Building Society in Commercial Street, Halifax.

diesel engine that was used to power a mortar mill and plant for crushing waste and lower grade stone which was used as aggregate. The youngest member of the Crawshaw line, William Crawshaw's great grandson Mark Crawshaw, has devoted his spare time to putting the old equipment back in working order. Mark's elder sister, Lisa Amer, joined the family firm after graduating from Aston University and today helps her mother Jean to run the company's accounts and administration department.

Today the company concentrates on building work and the Castle Quarry site is no longer used for quarry operations. All raw material is bought in. In the early 1980s the company developed the joinery side of its business, first of all using premises behind the Northfield pub in Barkisland formerly owned by the village joiner Edwin Darby. In the late 1990s however an office and a new joinery workshop were built in Castle Quarries to make the business more efficient working from a single site.

Without the activities of the Crawshaw family Calderdale might indeed have been a very different place today.

Top left: *The extension of the Goat House Church at Rishworth School.* ***Left:*** *A new portico at Broadcarr House built in 2000.* ***Below:*** *Mark Crawshaw and the refurbished Blackstone diesel engine.*
Bottom: *From left to right, Alan Crawshaw, Graham Crawshaw, Jean Crawshaw, Mark Crawshaw and Lisa Amer (neé Crawshaw).*

Work today is generally within a 25 mile radius of Ripponden and still involves building one-off houses and commercial/industrial buildings together with domestic, commercial and industrial extensions and modifications. Key features of the firm's work are high quality cabinet work and traditional joinery made to measure, naturally all combined with masonry and general building work completed to a very high standard. For many years the company has also been sexton to around 20 church

being of Roman classical style - arches, columns and colonnades. The decline of the Piece Hall coincided with the transition of cloth production from the home to the factory, and the trustees handed it over to Halifax Corporation in 1868. The Piece Hall remains a centre for trade and recreation, but it is unlikely ever again to host the great Sunday School 'Jubilee Sings', the last one of which attracted 30,000 people in 1890.

Top: A lively scene of intense activity is highlighted by this 1930s shot across the cobbled courtyard of Halifax's Piece Hall. Old and new, in the shape of horses and carts and motorised vehicles, jostle for space, whilst bags and boxes of produce find protection under the 'lean to' buildings which have now disappeared.

Above: A busy day has probably just concluded at the Piece Hall in 1967, at which date it had served around a century as a wholesale fish, fruit and vegetable market. The 10,000 square yards of the courtyard look somewhat cluttered, and these buildings have now disappeared to give much freer movement across the cobbles when markets are not in progress. It is Halifax's good fortune that the Piece Hall survived the 1960s redevelopment mania, for in some towns fine old market halls were simply demolished rather than some attempt being made to integrate them into new struc-tures. As it happens the Piece Hall is now internationally famous as a unique survival of an eighteenth century cloth hall, recognition really growing after the cleaning and restoration programme of the early 1970s. The Piece Hall was opened in 1779 in order for local cloth makers to display their woollen 'pieces' for sale to national and international buyers. The Hall had 315 rooms around the courtyard, the design

The names of some of the traders are clearly visible, and might evoke a few memories for some people. This was the Piece Hall in full swing as a wholesale fish, fruit and vegetable market, although its original purpose had been to serve the thriving domestic cloth industry. The 10,000 square yards and 315 rooms of the Piece Hall had been opened in 1779 for local manufacturers and smaller cloth makers to display their 'pieces' for sale. By the nineteenth century, a mechanised factory age made the Piece Hall redundant. It was taken over by the local Corporation in 1868, and soon afterwards the produce market began. It was only when the wholesalers moved out, and the cleaning and restoration programme began in the early 1970s, that it was discovered what an archi-tectural gem lay beneath the accumulated grime. Since then the Piece Hall has formed a centre for small shops, markets, concerts and special events, whilst some visitors simply marvel at the imposing Classical arches and colonnades.

We'll be fans forever

From its modest beginnings Halifax Fan Limited has always been a dedicated fan manufacturer specialising in the design and manufacture of centrifugal fans and continues to expand it's product range. The company has come a long way to acquire the status it holds today. It demonstrates, by virtue of an impressive factory and office complex, that hard work, consistency of purpose and personal commitment can and does succeed in the UK's manufacturing industry today.

It was 1965 when the company first started the manufacture of Centrifugal Fans, in the premises which were the old debtors' prison in Gaol Lane, in the town centre. Most of their work in those days came from the local carpet and textile mills, most of which are now long gone. The company was founded by David A Scott, a mechanical engineer who specialised in ductwork design and ventilating systems, together with two colleagues Brian Walker and Roy Taylor, who became directors. After coping with atrocious working conditions for fifteen months the company moved to larger rented premises at Boothtown, where they stayed for almost six years until a move in 1972 to their present location at Mistral Works, Salterhebble.

Halifax Fan invests heavily in the training and development of it's staff and an apprentice training scheme ensures not only a constant supply of highly skilled production staff but also a strong and very experienced management team. Many of today's senior personnel originally joined the company as apprentices or in junior positions. The present managing director, Charles Rodley, joined the company as a draughtsman but very quickly demonstrated his management skills and in 1974 was promoted to General Manager.

From the very beginning Halifax Fan has been proud to design, develop and build it's products in Halifax. Everything originates from their own designs and nothing

Above left: David Scott, founder. **Below:** *Celebrating the delivery of a second CNC Nibbling machine in 1980.* **Bottom:** *Elizabeth Peacock, JP, MP on her visit to Halifax Fan in 1990 for their 25 year celebration.*

is made under license or copied. The range developed and includes designs such as the simple paddle blade, multi vane forward curved, backward inclined fan, blower and exhauster fans. The names that go with them - Chinook, Beaufort, Mercury and Mistral amongst others, are all names well established for setting standards of reliability and performance throughout the industry.

In addition to it's standard range of products Halifax Fan designs bespoke fans to meet specialist individual requirements. Some of the more unusual problems that Halifax Fan's team has solved include the production of fans for machines which blow sugar coating onto pills, for lifting confectionery out of baking tins and for machines which pick peas and sprouts. It is this dynamism and creativity that helps Halifax Fan maintain it's competitive edge.

First class production resources have always been of prime importance and in the years since 1965 the company's manufacturing machinery and equipment has developed

Above: A selection of some of the wide range of Halifax Fans. Top: The premises today.

from oxyacetylene cutters, a set of rollers and a hand bender to the present state-of-the-art laser cutting machine. The resulting precision means that components are so accurately made that they can be assembled rather than fitted during final fan construction. Halifax fans do not vibrate - they are all dynamically balanced to very tight limits thanks to an Italian dynamic balancing machine. Precision production techniques like these ensure Halifax Fan's first class world wide reputation.

Computerisation was adopted early on thanks to David Scott's pioneering efforts some years ago with a Commodore Computer when he wrote his first programme for fan selection. Today the very latest CAD/CAM and CNC technology is used in the production of all Halifax Fans and every item is meticulously inspected to the stringent standards which earned the company the coveted and essential BS5750 Part I and subsequent ISO 9001 Quality Assurance Certificates. At the same time, this is backed by a continuing programme of research and development which is synonymous with Halifax Fan's commitment to constant improvement, innovation and customer service.

The company's extensive customer base reflects the comprehensive range of market sectors and applications. Fans are made for heavy industry, iron and steel, mining and quarry constructions, fans for warships and the motor car industry, for maggot factories and television studios to name but a few. Future plans include the expansion of this customer base to secure potential customers perhaps not aware of all Halifax Fan has to offer.

Halifax Fan's founder, David Scott who retired in 1996, can be proud of all the company has achieved since its inception in 1965. From serving just the local industry the company has developed a world-wide reputation for the design and manufacture of high quality centrifugal fans.

Vintage textiles

The words 'textiles' and 'Halifax' are inseparable. For centuries the various processes associated with spinning yarn and weaving the yarn into bolts of cloth have been a primary occupation of the people of the Hebble and Calder valleys, and of the hills which overlook them. Some of the industrial enterprises in the area have origins going back to the beginning of the 19th century or even earlier, whilst others, making full use of the area's long industrial traditions, are of slightly more recent vintage such as the Waxman International based in Elland.

Albert Waxman founded A Waxman (Fibres) Ltd in 1958 setting himself up as a synthetic fibre merchant with offices in Bradford, first in Town Hall Chambers before moving to Cornwall House in 1960 as the business began to expand. In 1966 he acquired Grove Mills in Elland when his firm bought the businesses of both S Firth & Co Ltd and Synthetic Fibres Ltd converters, merchants, 'garnetters' and processors of man-made fibres, easily consolidating his business with theirs.

In 1968 the firm of Fibre Products Ltd of Bingley, specialising in the manufacture of moulding powders and decorative flock, was also added to the group.

The Waxman family's involvement in textiles however goes back to well before the 1930s when Albert Waxman's father in law, Mr A Sobol, arrived in Bradford after leaving his home in Leipzig to escape Nazi persecution. Mr Sobol was a prosperous wool merchant and soon established a successful business in England's leading wool centre.

Above left: *An early advertisement.* ***Below:*** *The laying of the foundation stone of the Denholme premises by Mrs Waxman.* ***Bottom:*** *Mr and Mrs Waxman in a picture dating from August 1962.*

In 1950 Albert Waxman joined the Sobol firm and began to specialise in synthetic fibres before eventually setting up on his own and in due course moving to Elland and Grove Mill.

Nothing however runs smoothly forever. A disastrous fire destroyed the main Grove Mill in March 1970; since then four major new buildings have been erected on the site by Marshall Construction Ltd of Elland, totalling approximately 100,000 square feet. Out of the 1970 fire emerged a new factory designed to take advantage of the most modern methods of handling and processing synthetic materials, a factory considered at the time to be the most modern garnetting plant in the whole country.

Albert Waxman's son Richard joined the firm in 1976. After several years Richard became managing director of Waxman International, taking over responsibility for the company's important Japanese connection of marketing highly specialised

modacrylic fibre and in the meantime obtaining the sole selling rights for the fibre throughout Europe.

Richard subsequently founded the business of Waxman Ceramics which imports and distributes ceramic tiles and mosaics throughout the UK, serving both the contract and domestic sectors. The company would eventually become the UK's leading supplier to the swimming pool construction industry and be the UK's largest importer of mosaics. In 1990 a purpose built warehouse was erected on the Grove Mill site to accommodate these two important businesses.

Today the Waxman Group Ltd employs more than 50 staff. Whilst Albert Waxman remains Chairman of Waxman Holdings, Richard Waxman has effectively taken over the running of the business and created the successful Waxman Group Ltd, of which he is Chairman.

After more than 50 years the Waxman Group has come a long way since its modest beginnings in a small, office in Bradford. Today the business is multifaceted embracing not just man-made textiles but also ceramics and wine - and no doubt further diversification will occur in the future. The history of Calderdale is replete with the stories of business which have evolved to meet changing circumstances, those that have not changed having soon fallen by the wayside; of one thing we can be certain, today the future of the Waxman Group Ltd looks as promising as its past.

Above left: *Mr Albert Waxman with Mr Takeda, now President of the Kaneka Corporation and his family.*
Top: *Grove Mills in a view from 1990.*

Prepared for scholastic enlightenment

Continuing a tradition of educational excellence which goes back nearly a century, Lightcliffe Preparatory School is known as a happy place in which to learn, many children join through recommendation. The school caters for around 160 pupils ranging from two-year-olds in the nursery through to eleven-year-olds preparing for the big change of going to secondary school. Emphasis is laid on a formal education with a high priority given to literacy and numeracy, though a varied education is offered through a wide range of musical, craft and physical activities.

The building in which the school is housed was originally built in 1886 to be the home of Hipperholme and Lightcliffe Liberal Club. During 1914 this was dissolved following an extraordinary meeting of the committee and the premises were managed by the trustees who agreed to lease the upstairs rooms of the building as a school to Miss Field who took up residence in 1915. In the early years the school was managed and run by two teachers - Miss Field herself and Miss Price. They taught their charges of whom there were around twenty, to be 'ladies' and 'gentlemen'. Children started at the school when they were 6, at first during the mornings only, staying all day when they were older. Fees were three guineas a term and the children were taught sums, French verbs and painting, singing and dancing. There was no playground so children stayed in the building and drank milk at 1d per bottle.

School meals were not available in these early days and many pupils went home for lunch. But if bad weather prevented them from doing that there was the tuck shop on Wakefield Road which sold boiled eggs.

The second world war brought many changes to life across the country and Miss Field's High School, Lightcliffe, as it was known, underwent a change of use to a canteen, known as a British Restaurant, giving refuge to many local residents. It could seat 132 people at one sitting. The first midday meal prepared in the kitchens there consisted of pea soup, roast beef, potatoes and cabbage with jam roll or rice pudding to follow. In 1948 it was partly utilised as a municipal school canteen. The school later became known as, The High School, Lightcliffe.

Archibald Lionel Watkins (The grandfather of the school's present Principal, purchased the school in 1955 with a mortgage of £2,000 from the Halifax Building Society. Mr Watkins ran the school, purchasing the neighbouring field from Mr White of 2 Highland Ville in 1958. This quickly became the school's playground and was no doubt greatly appreciated by the children. Archibald's son, Philip Watkins and his wife, Joan, took over the ownership

Top: *The 'High School' as it was in the 1950s.*
Above: *Staff pictured in the 1950s, Archibald Watkins is seated in the centre with his wife, Maud, on his right.* **Left:** *Archibald Watkins.*

Catering facilities have come a long way since the days when a boiled egg was available from the local tuck ship - now a range of balanced and nutritious meals are cooked and served on the premises.

The school is looking forward to the future with confidence. Staff are approaching the future with enthusiasm and feel that the next years will be an exciting time for the school and, thanks to their dedication and commitment, they will be able to continue offering pupils the highest possible standard of education.

Above: An early class of pupils. *Left:* The school as it looked at the end of the 1990s. *Below:* Boys enjoying Rugby, one of the many sports now taught at the school.

of the school when Archibald died in 1972. When they retired in 1979 they transferred the ownership of the school to their daughter, Mrs Jacky A Pickersgill, herself a former pupil, who runs the school to this day.

The school has a policy of maintaining small classes, normally around twenty which enables tuition to be conducted on a very personal level. Children of all abilities are accepted at the school and pride is taken in its close links with Hipperholme Grammar School. Each child's progress and development is closely monitored.

Classrooms are bright and well equipped, enabling Lightcliffe to blend 'traditional' teaching methods with the best of modern techniques. Classwork is regularly complemented by visits to places of historical and geographical interest.

Wired up for success

Dixon's of Halifax Ltd was originally founded in 1928, under the name of J Arthur Dixon, when Arthur and his father-in-law joined resources and formed a company together. For several years they traded in wire goods and butchers' sundries, like meat skewers hooks and ticket pins, which were all produced by hand methods. During the mid 1920s Arthur Dixon joined the Siddal & Hilton group of companies, who already had a number of factories in the Halifax area trading in wire products. The Dixon business moved into small components manufacture and developed into automatic machinery making it one of the most modern factories of its day. The firm moved to its present Raglan Street premises in the 1930s.

The second world war had a dramatic effect on the company, because it gained government contracts and Dixons started to expand, this prompted them to move increasingly into automated production. The company has always relied extensively on its highly skilled toolmakers for the production of all its in-house tools. In a typical year over 950 different types were produced and it is a company boast that they are able to turn their hand to any requirement the customer may have.

During the second world war the company contributed to the war effort by manufacturing wire parts for bedsteads, precision springs, mine markers, rubber

dinghy fittings, ammunition box hinges and clips, Piat sling swivels, water bottle cork pins, mess can handles, fittings for Morrison shelters, rings and pins for hand grenades, welded fittings for equipment, and tent pegs among other things.

A document in the company archives from around that time shows the company to be trading from its present premises, The Victoria Wire Works in Raglan Street, Halifax, comprising a 'Modern Building on One Floor'. It had a total of 59 employees, nine in the office in administration and sales, seven skilled men, 38 semi-skilled people (of whom 25 were women), and five unskilled workers. At that time five per cent of production was sent directly for export with a further 60 per cent going for indirect export, the remaining 35 per cent was marked down as being for the 'Home Market and Government Orders'.

Above: *Girls at work in the factory.* **Right:** *An early advertisement for Arthur Dixon & Co Ltd.* **Far Right:** *The factory in the early 1930s.*

parts for mixers and hooks for spring balances.

In 1985 Dixons became one of the first wire component manufacturers to attain BS5750 Part 2 registration. In 1989 the Siddal and Hilton group sold Dixons to the Pullamflex International Group and the company developed into a major supplier to the automotive industry and expanded into wire fabricating and plastic coated goods. They are skilled in working with a variety of materials, Mild Steel, Spring Steel, Aluminium, Brass, Copper and Phosphor Bronze.

In 1994 Dixons became independent for the first time in 60 years and have experienced a period of sustained growth and development since that time.

They are committed to meeting the needs of their customers in quality, service and reliability and to achieving and maintaining world class standards of excellence, and are poised to continue their success in the future.

*Top left: An interior view of the factory. **Above right:** Bus advertising in the 1960s. **Above left:** An early letterhead. **Below:** Peter Bottomley receiving the BS5750 Certificate from Mr Albert Thayre, Vice Chancellor of Bradford University, far right, with Adrian Shaw, left and Peter Siddall of SH Wire and Tube products, second left, in 1986.*

An extensive range of components are produced for the building and construction industry including clips for use on suspended ceilings, clips to hold tiles in position on roofs, pipe clips, chairs for reinforcing wire in floors, ceilings and walls and formwork for various concrete applications.

The start of the 1960s saw the firm having to comply with shorter working week agreements negotiated by the Engineering and Shipbuilders Unions. These saw the 44 hour working week reduced to 42 hours. The document, outlining the new arrangements, is fascinating for the insight it gives to the attitudes to work observed at a time when the majority of the workforce still vividly recalled the hardship and austerity of the war time conditions. There was 'The necessity of maintaining a strict observance of the working hours at all times' because 'time wasting factors are injurious to the well-being and prosperity of the Industry'. The new (shorter) working week at Dixons was to be as follows, 7.30 am to 12 o'clock, 12.45 pm to 4-45 pm (4-15 on Friday).

The firm manufactures components for household industries and include such a diverse range of parts as spirals for whisks, springs for vacuum cleaners,

Providing the right sparks in a competitive industry

An Electrician is a well known occupation today but more than half a century ago   L Tyson Electrical Contractors was plying a trade still very much in its infancy. Founded not long after the second world war by Mr Leslie Tyson in 1948, the original business began at The Stubbin, Triangle, Sowerby Bridge. Leslie was brought up in Sheffield where his parents ran a wholesale and retail tobacconists; hard work and a strong business ethic surrounded his early life. Before starting the business he served with the Royal Engineers Bomb Disposal Unit and later as an Electrician for an electrical firm in Sheffield.

After the war electricity supplies were only just beginning to be installed in rural areas. Demand was high due to society's rapid uptake of this modern day energy source. This was particularly the case in the Ryburn valley, where Leslie was sent to work by his employers. During this time he met and married his wife, Margaret, and realising the demand for electrical work from homes in the area, decided to relocate and start his own firm of Electrical Contractors there. He felt that as demand continued to

Above: Leslie and Margaret on their wedding day.
Below: Early company vehicle with Leslie and young son, Nigel - L Tyson & Son.

increase, starting a business of this sort would prove to be very lucrative, or at least provide a steady living and income for those involved.

Over the years L Tyson's has remained very much a family firm. In the beginning Leslie Tyson was the electrical contractor and his wife Margaret handled the administration and the accounts. Leslie was officially approved in 1960 by The National Inspection Council For Electrical Installation Contractors and was given the then prestigious, now essential, Certificate of Enrolment as proof of his skills. In the early 60s the scope of the firm was widened to include plumbing and heating.

From 1967 sons Nigel and Lloyd Tyson joined the firm and trained as Electricians; in 1981 Nigel's wife, Carolyn also joined. The firm became known as L Tyson & Sons. After Leslie's retirement in 1981, due to ill health, eldest son Nigel took over the business and has run it ever since. Margaret Tyson also retired from the business not long after, in 1989.

The company remained at The Stubbin until expansion forced a move to their present location at Chapelfields Mill, Elland Road, Ripponden, Sowerby Bridge. The tools and materials used have not altered a great deal over the years and the basic methods of work are still applicable.

The company has kept the high reputation it holds today because of a very personal business philosophy. This involves hard work and 'keeping a personal finger on the button'. A traditional concept, this is the company's way of doing things, and none the worse for it, either. An abiding feature of a by-gone era is the personal touch, the care and attention to detail taken when practicing one's trade. This is one aspect of the 'Good Old Days' worth hanging on to. The company also prides itself on its close relationship with staff and even has one second generation employee, whose father trained with the firm in the 1950s. This again reflects the company's personal approach to work.

L Tyson & Sons has now been in business for more than half a century, and this is, in no mean amount, due to a love of the trade. This helps to keep the company fresh after all these years; new ideas constantly improving work practices, whilst never neglecting the tried and tested traditional approach. There is no need to drastically alter the company, their business philosophy clearly works; customers use L Tyson's time after time because of the high quality of service they receive. The company is living proof that their way of doing things has been extremely popular to generations of customers. No doubt it will still remain popular for many years to come.

Changes that have occurred are due to the advent of PVC materials and electronic testing equipment, the latter helping enormously with ensuring the safety of installations. Of course, there have been a great many changes in automobiles; today's vans look quite different to some of their earlier models.

The years of experience in the industry L Tyson has acquired, stands the company in good stead for maintaining loyal support and a strong customer base. The company does not advertise, it relies upon its reputation as a long running family business and on contacts established over many years. The main markets for L Tyson are prefabricated and modular building system end users; customers are generally health authorities, education institutions, MOD and Councils. Continued expansion is planned for the future, incorporating new clients.

Top left: Clare Tyson and the family business in Sheffield.
Top Right: Leslie Tyson as a boy.
Above: The certificate awarded to L Tyson in 1960 by the National Inspection Council for Electrical Installation Contracting.

Dressed for work

Where might you buy a chef's hat, a white lab coat or a nurse's dress in Halifax? It is possible to buy not only these diverse items but many other items of work clothing from a single source - if you know where to look.

It is not too long ago that pyjamas and thick underwear were a necessity rather than a matter of personal choice. Halifax's Beech Tree (Manufacturing) Ltd based at Beech Tree Mills in Raglan Street traces its origins back to the dark days of the first world war in 1916 when a partnership was formed to manufacture cosy underwear and warm pyjamas to meet the needs of the day.

In the years following the ending of the Great War in 1918, until after the end of the second world war in 1945, a chain of retail shops was built up selling what we now think of as old fashioned wrap around pinnies of the kind we associate in our minds with Coronation Street's Hilda Ogden, as well as budget dresses for the working woman.

On the back of the post-war economic boom the chain of shops was expanded during the 1950s, 60s and 70s peaking at 36 branches. Throughout that period all the goods sold in the shops were manufactured in Halifax.

Since its origins back in 1916 the firm had remained in family hands. In 1987 however the original owners sold the firm and control passed to new owners.

In the light of subsequent events the family owners must have been relieved to have got out when they did. Initially trade continued to do

Right (both pictures): *Different stages in the manufacture of garments at Beechtree.*

very well in the retail boom of the late 1980s, but in the early part of the 1990s that economic boom had turned to bust and the firm entered some difficult and turbulent years.

Sales began to fall and the business had to begin selling off its shops. The firm's problems culminated in a voluntary agreement having to be reached with creditors in 1996 - an event which the firm has now fortunately put well behind it.

Whilst many firms facing similar problems might well have gone under the owners of Beech Tree determined to survive. As a result of the difficulties it faced the business was thoroughly reorganised:

tation of both staff and a business are at stake. At Beech Tree every effort is made to maintain prices at a realistic level with garments that are big on quality, represent great value and both fit well and look smart.

For cutting the firm works from computer generated patterns for pinpoint accuracy, with garments assembled by a skilled team of seamstresses. Garments are stitched with polyester core spun thread, not a cheaper alternative, with bartacks on all stress points, whilst each pocket top and opening is reinforced to take the stresses of heavy day to day use. Every

all the shops were sold off or closed whilst direct selling by catalogue, and telesales was expanded eventually providing a period of substantial growth, reaching cumulative levels of 30 per cent per annum.

The range of products sold was expanded with the target market today being cleaning companies, health care, large multiple retail chains, nursing agencies and light industry.

The stocked range of standard merchandise and stock for specific large customers now amounts to half a million pounds worth, or 80,000 garments, held on the premises, with next day service for quality merchandise supplied by friendly helpful staff.

One third of today's supplies come from the Halifax factory, a third from Poland and the remainder outsourced from other suppliers.

Choosing the right work-wear for ones employees is important as the image, comfort, safety and presen-

garment made in the Halifax factory is examined by experienced inspectors; they are instructed 'if you wouldn't buy it yourself then don't sell it'.

The firm has come a long way since the pyjama and underwear business founded in the middle of the first world war; it has seen some difficult times which many businesses would have failed to survive. Today in the opening years of the second millennium Beech Tree has found its second wind and now looks set for a future as prosperous as its past.

Above (both pictures): *Examples of the finished product.* ***Right:*** *Michael Uttley, Managing Director.*

A magic carpet ride to dreams come true

'Dean Clough must now be one of the most remarkable new centres of enterprise and artistic endeavour in the country.' This was the view of 'The Independent' columnist Paul Vallery recently and few would disagree with him. This huge 19th century complex in the centre of Halifax used to reverberate to the clatter of carpet weaving looms when it was home to John Crossley & Sons, at one time the largest carpet manufacturer in the world. Today it is once again a hive of activity housing numerous businesses and a site for many artistic endeavours - though considerably easier on the eardrums. It has become an inspiration and example of what can be done with old buildings which have intimate connections with the locality, and proof that a town does not have to destroy its local architectural landmarks to meet the demands of twenty-first century people.

In 1983 after the closure of Crossley's Carpets, the musician and entrepreneur Ernest Hall and his son Jeremy bought the site. Major companies like The Halifax and Royal & SunAlliance have made their homes in the complex, together with numerous start-up companies that have either developed on site or moved on as their business expanded. Today, more than 100 companies are based at Dean Clough employing over 3,500 people between them. A major programme of restoration and development has seen the site transformed from near

Above: Sir Ernest Hall. ***Right:*** *A ram's eye view of Dean Clough.* ***Below:*** *A dramatic view of Dean Clough from the Burdock Way flyover.*

In addition to arts and business activities, more and more visitors to Dean Clough come for the growing number of retail businesses. These range from the award winning Design House Restaurant and the Viaduct Gallery Café, to the Design House Shop which offers a wide range of Ceramics, Jewellery and household fixtures and fittings (most of which is inspired by young contemporary designers). New and exciting additions have been the Fitness First gymnasium and the recently opened Travelodge hotel; yet more evidence of the regeneration of these great buildings which are inexorably linked with the history of Halifax.

Dean Clough is a place where many artistic and commercial dreams are realised, perhaps in line with its founder's experience. Sir Ernest Hall recently stated 'I have discovered that the more impossible our ambitions, the more achievable they become'.

dereliction to high grade commercial property. With more of the site still to be developed it is thought that the Dean Clough site will eventually employ more people than it ever did as a carpet factory.

At the same time the Halls have pursued a policy of combining commerce with the arts and education. Besides eight galleries and a theatre, Dean Clough has attracted a variety of charities, including the Design Dimension Educational Trust, The Henry Moore Studio, various theatre companies, arts, music and media groups, and the Dean Clough artists - a 24 strong co-operative of visual artists, many of them internationally recognised.

As a venue for Music and Theatre, Dean Clough hosts many concerts throughout the year ranging from Jazz to classical music. During the Spring of 2000 Ted Hughes' last play 'Alcestis' premiered in Dean Clough's Viaduct Theatre to critical acclaim. The production by the Dean Clough based Northern Broadsides Theatre Company fulfilled the wishes of Hughes, the late Poet Laureate that Alcestis should be first staged in the Calder valley, the place of his birth.

*Top left: The Upstairs Gallery. **Above left:** Rehearsals under way for a production at the Viaduct Theatre, Dean Clough. **Above right:** The Foyer. **Below:** Travelodge, the latest addition to the Dean Clough complex.*

A crowd of excited children and adults await the arrival of King George VI and Queen Elizabeth when they visited Brighouse on October 20th 1937.

Acknowledgments

Stephen Gee

Calderdale MBC Community Services Department, Shibden Hall, Halifax.

Mr and Mrs Harry Ludlam OBE

Lyndon Reeve

Polly Salter, Social History Officer, Shibden Hall Museum

John T Hirst

Chris Hirst

Peter Bridge

Mrs E Naylor

Thanks are also due to
Peter Thomas who penned the editorial text
and Steve Ainsworth and Judith Dennis for their copywriting skills